PERMISSION
To SPEND

Tom Wall, Ph.D.

PERMISSION *To* SPEND

Maximize Your Retirement with the
Best Kept Secret in Personal Finance

Published by Best Seller Publishing®, St. Augustine, FL
Best Seller Publishing® is a registered trademark.
Printed in the United States of America.

ISBN:978-1-959840-21-3

For more information, please write:
Best Seller Publishing®
53 Marine Street
St. Augustine, FL 32084
or call 1 (626) 765-9750
Visit us online at: www.BestSellerPublishing.org

Contents

Introduction
You Will Be Afraid to Spend

Let me repeat that—you will be afraid to spend.

If you're reading this book, you've probably at least considered how much you need to save for retirement. You've thought about what your "number" is. You're putting money into your 401(k) up to the amount your employer matches, perhaps even overfunding that account or saving additional money elsewhere. If you're really good, you've even done the homework on asset allocation and how to invest for the long run, without letting emotion get the best of you. And if you're among the very best, you're properly insured against the risk of dying, becoming disabled or enduring a significant period of unemployment before you reach those golden years.

But no matter who you are, you most likely don't have an answer to the following question: When you arrive at retirement's doorstep with whatever sum of money you were able to accumulate, how much of it will you be able to spend each year? Put differently, you probably only have an accumulation strategy. What's your spending strategy?

Millions of Americans are under-enjoying their retirements right now because they're afraid to spend. They're afraid of what will happen if they outlive their assets. They're afraid of what will happen if they require expensive ongoing medical care—care that can quickly cost hundreds of thousands of dollars and isn't covered by any medical plan. They're afraid of what will happen if they need access to significant amounts of cash later in life for unforeseen circumstances. And those with children or strong ties to their community are concerned about the financial legacy they're leaving behind. The bottom line is, they're worried about running out of money, and in response they are spending as little as possible, living well below the lifestyle their assets should be able to provide.

Don't be one of these people. These people are victims. They are victims of an investment industry that taught them the rules of how to *A*-ccumulate but failed to disclose that many of those very rules work against their *DE*-cumulation strategy. They are victims of a generational shift that replaced pension plans with investment accounts, which completely transferred the risks to the individual. And they are woefully unaware of and unprepared for those risks, which is why they live scared and hoard money, just in case those unlikely risks become their reality.

I wrote this book because I am a leading expert in one of the financial industry's best-kept secrets—and the answer to this problem. In my 20 years of working with thousands of financial advisors, I can confidently assert that no more than a tiny fraction of them fully understand it. However, through a modern twist on a centuries-old product, one can confidently build a strategy to spend and enjoy that which has taken a lifetime to accumulate.

Before I get to the solution, you're going to need some background. I'll begin by discussing conventional wisdom along with many tried and true financial principles of generating wealth. Think of this section as Retirement Planning 101—a general guide to make sure you're on the right track. I'll then talk about the major risks to your retirement and what will hold you back. You'll get an in-depth lesson on withdrawal strategies and how market forces can impact your decisions. With this foundation in place, you'll then discover strategies to unlock the value of your financial assets and realize their full potential in the most efficient manner possible. At the end, I'll discuss what to look for when seeking an advisor and the method I use to grant clients "permission" to spend.

WHY I CARE SO MUCH

I was 24 years old when we got the news: my mother had cancer, and it had already spread throughout her body. The news was surreal, and the diagnosis was terminal. It was quite likely too late. But we all kept our chins up, most of all my mother, who turned out to be a stronger woman than I ever could have imagined. We knew there was always a chance and that she'd fight as hard as she could.

It was March, and I was recently engaged with plans to marry the following spring. Mom wasn't supposed to make it that long, so we moved the wedding to August. Over the next several months, I watched my mother struggle through treatments and everything that comes when you're fighting for your life. I would occasionally drive her to the hospital and run errands when needed, thrilled to fractionally repay her for all she'd done for me over the course of my life. In the process, we had discussions like never before and became closer than ever. We were never much of a touchy-feely family, but we all started to say "I love you" and hug more frequently.

The clock was our enemy, but in this amazing way, it was also our friend. It shaped my future relationships with my father, sister and extended family. I was able to dance with my mother at my wedding and make memories over the subsequent holiday season that I'll never forget. Shortly after that, about a year after first getting her diagnosis, I had the hardest night of my life as I held my mother's hand and experienced her passing away at the age of 54. She missed out on what was to be an amazing, affluent, world-traveling retirement with her high school sweetheart—a hard-earned reward for decades of work, business travel, saving and sacrifice.

At the time all of this was happening, I was a young financial advisor trying my hardest to make it in a very difficult industry. I was focused on learning as fast as I could, quickly obtaining advanced licenses and credentials to prove I knew what I was talking about. I was taught all the rules of thumb and basic principles to accumulate wealth and insure against the tragedies that can derail those plans. More importantly, I was also taught how to ask great questions and uncover the hopes and dreams of my clients. My advice would then serve as the recipe to make those dreams come true financially. However, one thing began to bother me, and I carried that with me throughout the rest of my career.

All of these assumptions, best practices, rules of thumb and tips for accumulating wealth rested on the expectation of a long retirement. They also maximized enjoyment of money at old ages, often requiring great sacrifice along the way. To me this seemed unfair, inefficient and highly risky because you might not actually make it. And even if you did, you might not be physically capable of enjoying it the way you could at a younger age. While most healthy retirees will live into their 80s and beyond, many will not.

If these folks have deferred enjoyment of that wealth their entire life, then it could go to waste. Sure, loved ones would inherit it, but that was not the stated goal of that saving and sacrifice. As a smart guy who loves puzzles, I turned my focus toward figuring out how to maximize one's ability to spend at younger, healthier ages, while still following the fundamentals of financial planning.

In the years that followed, I watched a close relative receive a similar diagnosis and pass away in her early 40s, leaving two young children behind. One of my closest friends from college died suddenly of a heart attack as I was writing this book. My grandfather made it to retirement but died at age 70, before he could fully enjoy the fruits of a 45-year career. There, unfortunately, isn't much we can do regarding tragedies, except to make sure there is ample life insurance coverage for the surviving family. However, there absolutely are ways to help retirees maximize their early spending so they can enjoy their lives and accumulated wealth to the fullest degree.

QUALIFIED TO BE YOUR GUIDE

I have a PhD in retirement income planning and conducted original research under the advisement of some of the most prolific researchers and authors in the field. Throughout my 20-year career in financial planning, I've had the honor and privilege to learn from the industry's smartest minds as I earned a master of science in financial services, a master of business administration, a bachelor of arts in economics and two industry-leading designations: Chartered Life Underwriter (CLU), and Chartered Financial Consultant (ChFC). Academic curiosity and advising from a place of honor and integrity have always driven me to leave no difficult question unanswered.

Professionally, I have held numerous roles in the financial services industry. Starting as an award-winning financial advisor, I subsequently moved up the ranks as a product expert at a Fortune 100 financial services company, presenting to and consulting with thousands of advisors and company leaders. My time at that company culminated in a senior leadership role in marketing. I oversaw a 19-person team of product-marketing professionals and worked behind the scenes with actuaries, product developers, attorneys, communications teams and sales leadership. I have been part of the decision-making process around product sustainability and maximizing the long-term value for policy owners. I have also gone toe to toe with the kinds of unscrupulous competitors and misleading marketing schemes that can give this important industry a black eye.

With 20 years of professional and academic experience, I have now refocused my career toward helping people like you understand the amazing benefits of what may be the most misunderstood and underappreciated assets the industry has to offer. Investments are sexy and fun to talk about, but the real magic in financial planning comes from crucial conversations around hopes, dreams and goals, and the things that are holding people back from achieving them. Alleviating fear and putting you in control is what *Permission to Spend* is all about.

CANNOT STRESS THIS ENOUGH
(IMPORTANT DISCLOSURES)

Do NOT employ any strategy or idea in this book without the guidance of a trusted, credentialed financial advisor.

The information in this book is intended to be general in nature, and not offered as specific advice to any individual. The book discusses life insurance in detail, but illustrated or projected policy values are hypothetical in nature and do not represent specific offerings of any company. Dividends are not guaranteed, and historical studies are based on third-party data. Furthermore, policy provisions discussed may not be available from all insurance companies. Individuals are encouraged to work with a properly licensed financial professional to obtain suitable recommendations.

The information provided is not written or intended as specific tax or legal advice. Insurance companies, their subsidiaries, employees and representatives are generally not authorized to give tax or legal advice. Individuals are encouraged to seek advice from their own tax or legal counsel.

This book discusses access to the cash value of whole life insurance policies for various purposes. It is important to note that access to cash values through borrowing or partial surrenders will reduce the policy's cash value and death benefit, increase the chance the policy will lapse, and may result in a tax liability if the policy terminates before the death of the insured. Additionally, it is important to understand that dividends available to owners of participating whole life policies are not guaranteed.

Any opinions presented in this book are of the author and do not represent the views of any financial institution. These opinions reflect the author's general experience, and the reader should not rely on those opinions for their own planning without the additional guidance of a properly licensed and credentialed financial professional.

Chapter 1
How Much Do You Need?

Early in my career, I met with a contractor named Dave who was completely overwhelmed and nervous about how much he and his wife, Lisa, would need for retirement. Dave and Lisa felt behind. They had focused heavily on their family, and Lisa had only recently returned to work after years of staying home to raise the children. With meager savings, financial independence seemed an impossibility. How could they ever retire? Would they have to work into their 70s? Could they? It all just seemed overwhelming.

WHAT'S YOUR RETIREMENT NUMBER?

Make no mistake, this is a BIG question and you simply cannot know the answer. The number I'm referring to, of course, is how much you need in your retirement account to feel comfortable telling your boss where he or she can shove things before you sail off into the sunset. If you think in purely theoretical terms, the ideal retirement spending strategy would be one that spreads income across your retirement based on your spending goals, and that has you spend your last dollar on your last day on earth, while leaving behind whatever financial legacy you would like. Why is this so hard to figure out? Try to answer these variables:

- What will your annual investment returns be in retirement?
- In what order will those annual returns occur?
- How long will you live?
- How long will your spouse live?
- Will either of you encounter any health shocks that require expensive ongoing care?
- What will the inflation rate be?
- What will you want to spend each year?
- How will the government tax your income?
- What is your Social Security strategy?
- Do you expect the government to pay Social Security and Medicare benefits as planned?
- Will you have charitable interests or a desire to leave money to children?
- Will there be a pandemic or political unrest that threatens every assumption above?

You get the idea.

Those are just some of the easy ones, and you can see why only sophisticated financial-planning software with a lot of assumptions about the answers to those questions could possibly solve the problem. In reality, however, it can't. Even if using historically conservative assumptions, the way we live and the way financial markets behave in the future may be very different. Some software, instead of relying on assumptions, will conduct thousands of simulations of future events based on historical experience, so that clients can choose a "probability of success" they are comfortable with.

For example, software may say that 90% of the time, your retirement spending strategy would have been successful based on events that were encountered in the past. But this assumes that we've seen all of the possible outcomes, which of course we have not. More importantly, any projected scenario that has failure (running out of money) as a significant possibility should be viewed as unacceptable. The reason is that running out of money at a very advanced age would potentially be catastrophic because that retiree is unlikely to be able to regain employment.

The key to a somewhat predictable retirement is mitigating the major risks and planning to be flexible in your spending. Elimination of all risks is not possible, but the biggest ones can be rendered far less threatening by using insurance and thoughtful allocation of assets. The next chapter will cover a lot of this. So, what's your number? The math is actually pretty simple; it's the variables (assumptions) that are the moving parts.

Step One: Determine your desired starting income

How much annual income (in today's dollars) do you want, within reason? Don't forget that your desired discretionary spending early in retirement may actually be *higher* than it was when you were spending most of your week not having fun. A common misconception is that someone can live on less than their pre-retirement income after the mortgage has been paid off and the children have moved out—but think carefully. When you're no longer going to the office every day, you may eat out more often, travel more and take part in recreational activities, all of which adds up. Every day in retirement could be like a weekend is for you now.

If you're unsure about how much income you'll really need, a good start may be to plan on using 100% of your current income, because many of the expenses you *need* to pay for today will be replaced by things you *want* to spend money on in retirement. Do you want to travel the world? Eat at the finest restaurants? Join the best country club? Or will you be content just enjoying the simple things and staying close to home? The answer to these questions will dictate roughly how much you will need to get started. Creating a detailed budget can help you zero in on that number.

Step Two: Determine your AQ

Your spending pattern in retirement will have a dramatic impact on how much you can safely begin spending. In step one, if you envisioned your retirement being filled with wanderlust as a social butterfly, the income you will need early in retirement is likely to be much higher than the income you will need later in retirement. This is because that kind of spending falls into the discretionary category, which on average tends to decline as people age and naturally spend less time and money on grand experiences.

Retirement has been described as occurring in three phases: the go-go years, the slow-go years and the no-go years. This concept is a nod to the reality that, as we age, we are physically less able and typically less motivated to travel and spend like we did during our younger years. Numerous studies of spending patterns from the Health and Retirement Study and the Consumer Expenditure Surveys have provided strong evidence that this is true, particularly among higher income earners. This is because fixed costs of living tend to represent a much higher percentage of income for those of lower means. Less of their spending is discretionary (for travel, dining, recreation, luxury brands and so on), so they're less able to adapt. On the other hand, those with greater levels of discretionary spending can cut back on those expenses. Health care is the one category that does tend to rise with one's age, but the direction of that rise is more like a hockey stick, with relatively level costs throughout retirement until the major health declines that traditionally impact those at older ages.

While necessary expenses (groceries, health care, housing) tend to remain level over time, discretionary expenditures fall as lifestyle moderates. So, if you have saved well and expect to be spending more early in retirement, worrying about your income inflating over time is probably not as necessary as you may have thought. Alternatively, if you are of modest means and expect to stay close to home as a result, a more conservative starting income may be prudent to weather potential market swings or inflationary environments. Furthermore, your ability to change your spending can have a profound impact on that starting income. If you have ample assets and discretionary expenses that can be curtailed, you can more easily manage your way through financial market swings. Think about what happened during the pandemic of 2020; many people got richer because they weren't out spending like they used to.

Retirement economists generally discuss spending in retirement in terms of an *initial withdrawal rate*: the percentage of your starting balance that you will take as income in your first year of retirement. Historically speaking, research has shown that one can safely begin spending about 4–6%

of their beginning retirement portfolios with a greater than 90% chance of not running out of money before they die. For those with less discretionary spending (and therefore a need for income to rise with inflation), starting with closer to a 4% withdrawal rate may be wise. But those with higher incomes and greater discretionary expenses could start with a much higher withdrawal rate and keep it level over time, with inflation slowly eating away the purchasing power of those dollars as lifestyle naturally declines. In the event of a market shock or an expensive health-care event, these folks are more able to adapt their spending each year. I call this one's AQ, or *adaptability quotient*. The more willing or able a retiree is to adjust spending as time goes by, the more they can spend up front. I discuss safe withdrawal rates in much greater detail in Chapter 5, along with a discussion of how changing market environments can dramatically impact results.

Step Three: Backward math

Now that you know roughly how much you'd like to initially live on and you have an idea of what your AQ is, we can do some math. All we need to do is divide your desired annual income from step one (in today's dollars) by the withdrawal rate you feel comfortable with (4% if conservative, and no more than 7% for the more aggressive).

So, putting it all together, let's say you determined you wanted $100,000 as your starting annual income. If your adaptability quotient puts you somewhere in the middle at a 5% withdrawal rate, that means you need about $2 million to comfortably retire without worrying about running out of money. That's your number! In today's dollars, that is.

Step Four: Adjust for inflation

Unless you're just about to retire, your number will need to be higher than what we just calculated due to inflation. Historically, the rate of inflation in the U.S. has been a mixed bag. But it has averaged about 3% over the last century. At the time of writing, reported inflation, post-pandemic, has been at the highest rate in 40 years. Whether that persists is anyone's guess, but its effect is to erode the purchasing power of your dollars. This means you'll need more of them in the future to buy the same amount of goods and services you can today. How that plays out is anyone's guess, but there are a couple of ways to approximate the effect. The first is a fun party trick to make you look like a genius to your math-averse friends, and the latter is a bit more accurate.

A rule of thumb called the "rule of 72" allows you to approximate how long it takes money to double based on an interest rate. Or, for inflation projections, you can use an assumed rate of inflation to determine how long it will take for the purchasing power of a dollar to be cut in half. For example, let's say we think inflation will be about 3% for the foreseeable future, which is roughly its historical average in the U.S. Dividing the number 72 by 3 gives us 24, meaning we can generally expect the cost of things to double in 24 years. Put differently, if you need $1 million to meet your lifestyle goals in retirement *today*, then in 24 years you'll need about $2 million to buy the same lifestyle. Figure 1.1 illustrates the potential results.

Inflation Rate	2%	3%	4%	5%	6%	7%	8%
Years Until Purchasing Power Is Cut in Half	36	24	18	14	12	10	9

Figure 1.1: The Rule of 72

Math for Shorter Time Frames

Based on the last exercise, if you are 24 years away from retirement, you can reasonably expect to need 2–3 times your number from step three in today's dollars, depending on how inflation actually unfolds. But if you're a bit closer to retirement, the rule of 72 probably isn't as helpful. Here's an idea of what to multiply your nest egg number (from step three) by, based on inflation expectations (if retirement years are becoming easier to envision).

Factors to multiply by at various inflation rates:

Years to Retirement	2%	3%	4%	5%	6%	7%	8%
5	1.10	1.16	1.22	1.28	1.34	1.40	1.47
10	1.22	1.34	1.48	1.63	1.79	1.97	2.16
15	1.35	1.56	1.80	2.08	2.40	2.76	3.17
20	1.49	1.81	2.19	2.65	3.21	3.87	4.66

Figure 1.2: Factors to multiply by at various inflation rates

So, putting it all together, let's say you want $100,000 of retirement income (in today's dollars) per year. We haven't discussed Social Security yet. But let's also assume about a quarter of your retirement income is covered by Social Security. In that case, we'd need $75,000 to cover the shortfall. If we assume that's 5% of the whole portfolio, we need about $1,500,000 to accomplish that goal today without worrying about running out of money. If retirement is about 10–15 years away, then that number may be about $2–3 million depending on how inflation changes things. Sound daunting? It doesn't have to be if you begin planning early. The first step is to understand how compound interest is your friend.

ACCUMULATING YOUR NUMBER

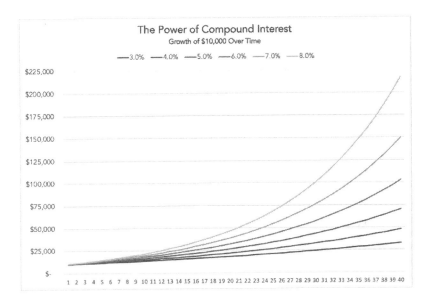

Figure 1.3: The Power of Compound Interest

The first thing you'll notice in the compound interest chart is the importance of your annual return. This is the reason nearly all financial advisors recommend significant exposure to the stock market and investments that have historically provided the greatest returns. These investments all carry risks, but a good financial advisor can help you mitigate those risks and stay within your comfort zone so you're not missing out.

The other less obvious thing is how much of those gains come at the end of the compound interest curve. In this example, $10,000 grows to just over $100,000 after 30 years at 8% growth per year. But if you look at the line and trace it back to when the account was half of that at $50,000, you'll see that over half of that growth occurred in just the last 9 years. This is the power of starting early with whatever you can.

So, two takeaways. The first is you must start now. Begin saving as much as you reasonably can today, and plan to increase that amount over time. Perhaps every time you get a raise at work, commit to saving half of that amount and living off of the other half. That's a great way to automatically increase savings and capture those raises instead of allowing "lifestyle creep" to lock in higher expenses going forward. "Pay yourself first" is a phrase you may have heard before, and it means that you must save each month like it's a bill you're paying to your future self. Additionally, aside from maybe your rent or mortgage, *you* should be your biggest bill. Don't let other debts or bills get in the way of your future financial freedom.

Another way to find money to save is to do an audit of your spending. I will never be the guy to tell you to stop ordering lattes every day if that's your little slice of joy each morning. This book is titled *Permission to Spend*, after all. But we live in a subscription economy now, where instead of major purchases we pay for things monthly, weekly and sometimes even daily. Those seemingly insignificant expenses really add up, and you might be surprised how many of them are for things you rarely use. Again, maybe conduct this exercise and invest half of what you save, while redirecting the other half of unnecessary expenses toward things you'll actually use to enhance your life.

To get started, there are great apps out there that allow you to link your financial accounts and credit cards. The apps will create an overall balance sheet that tells you where you stand. Some of them also help make projections for the future. Some will even examine your accounts for recurring payments that may no longer be serving you. My favorite is Personal Capital, which can be downloaded for free from any app store. Mint and NerdWallet are great alternatives as well.

The second takeaway is that you must minimize factors that erode your savings. Simply look at the difference in Figure 1.3 of earning 7% instead of 8%. That 1% difference in annual interest rate might not sound like much until you see that it results in 24% less saved for retirement! You're then spending only three-quarters of what you could have had if you had minimized expenses and maximized net returns. We'll discuss this in more detail in Chapter 2, but the main eroding factors are taxes, investment fees and market volatility.

Managing Costs

I have met very few clients who have a complete under-standing of how to minimize taxation over time. And that's the key—over time. The IRS has made it extremely difficult to avoid taxation on income today, but there are effective ways to manage it over the course of your investment life and even beyond, when assets pass to your beneficiaries. A good financial advisor can help you with this. Many people ask their tax professional or CPA for advice, but their profession tends to focus on minimizing current taxation, which isn't always in your best interest over the long haul. Make sure you sit down with an advisor who asks a lot of questions about your goals and vision for the future. In the business, we call these "fact versus feeling questions." The latter feeling questions." The latter is where the value is. The facts are the easy part.

Investment fees can also really cost you. According to the Investment Company Institute, the median 401(k) investor in 2018 paid around 0.94% in total fees. Remember how I showed you the power of a 1% difference in return? Well, your *actual* returns are all net of fees. The market does what it does, but if you can pay less in fees and get the same return, your net actual return will be higher. So how do you do that? Unfortunately, most people's largest investment asset is their retirement plan at work, where they have little control over fees. But there are two things you can do.

The first is to explore low-cost index fund options within the plan. Index funds have been demonstrated over and over to outperform more expensive traditional allocations that have much higher expense ratios. This is the whole "active versus passive" debate—which can lead you down a rabbit hole if you Google it—but for the common investor who is making modest, regular deposits over time, passive and inexpensive make all the sense in the world. That said, if the value of your investment portfolio has two commas and is largely outside your employer's retirement plan, you may qualify for unique opportunities that require high minimum investments but come with individualized service and management.

The second thing you can do (if your company is small enough) is lobby management to negotiate a better plan. The world is becoming more conscious of fees in general, and in many cases the plan provider can do better. In the end, just make sure you know what you're paying for. There is absolutely nothing wrong with paying management fees if you're getting a person in your corner to coach you along the way. If not, it may be time to take a critical look at how you can direct those fees toward your own future instead of the investment company's profit margin.

Now that you have an idea of how many millions you need to save for retirement, Figure 1.4 below shows you exactly how much to save monthly to accumulate $1 million. Simply look at the net rate of return you expect and how long you have until retirement. As you can see, taking more risk to get higher rewards—and minimizing how much goes out the door to fees—can really pay off over time and reduce how much you'll need to save. The key is to balance that risk with other complementary vehicles in your portfolio. I'll discuss this in further detail in Chapter 2.

Interest Rate	Years Until Retirement						
	10	15	20	25	30	35	40
2%	$7,522	$4,760	$3,387	$2,568	$2,026	$1,643	$1,359
4%	$6,769	$4,050	$2,717	$1,939	$1,436	$1,091	$843
6%	$6,072	$3,421	$2,154	$1,436	$991	$698	$500
8%	$5,430	$2,871	$1,686	$1,045	$667	$433	$285
10%	$4,841	$2,393	$1,306	$747	$439	$261	$157

Figure 1.4: How much to save per month to accumulate $1 million

All it took was some back-of-the-napkin math to get Dave and Lisa feeling in much greater control of their future. While the numbers still appeared daunting, they could see where the math came from and how to improve things over time. Maximizing compound interest and reducing eroding factors like taxes and fees would be their focus, while also figuring out ways to save as much as possible.

Chapter 2
Efficient Investing

It was 5:30 p.m. on a Tuesday, and I was out for drinks with some colleagues. A number I didn't recognize was ringing my phone, so I ignored it, assuming it was a telemarketer. The same number called three more times over the next 15 minutes, so I finally picked it up, thinking it might be an emergency call from someone I knew. "Tom, it's Steve. What's going on?!?" the voice on the other end said. "I just looked at my quarterly statement, and my account is down 20% since the last one! Should I be concerned? Should I sell? I didn't know this could happen. We need to meet ... Are you available tomorrow? I want out before it's too late!" My panicked client had never experienced a significant market downturn before and was clearly freaking out. He was considering abandoning his strategy at the worst possible time, and it was up to me to remind him what we were doing.

In professional auto racing, entire teams of engineers and technicians painstakingly examine every measurable detail of a car's performance to attempt to get an edge over the competition. The distribution of weight in the vehicle; the tires that are used in different environments; the type of oil that is used; how much fuel to carry at various points in the race and many other factors all contribute to a team's overall success. The compound effect of finding 1% improvements across all systems can add up to much greater efficiencies. In other sports, the goals are similar.

Bryson DeChambeau, the mad scientist of professional golf, has spent his career measuring every aspect of his swing on highly precise equipment to see where he could add incremental power. Slight changes to the angle at which his club hits the ground; the amount he pushes off his right leg; the arc of his swing; the length of the club shafts and countless other tweaks all combine to produce more power and accuracy for his swing. He also works with personal trainers to tailor his workouts for the strength and flexibility needed in certain muscle groups to efficiently produce power at all the right points in his swing. The result? He hits the ball farther than anyone else on the PGA Tour and was ranked No. 1 in the world in 2021.

In the sport of professional cycling, small tweaks to aerodynamics can provide that tiny edge needed to shave race-winning hundredths of a second off one's time. Alpine skiers measure the force applied during turns to make sure they're not unnecessarily losing speed. Regardless of the sport, with everyone playing by the same rules and with similar natural abilities, one must consistently seek incremental improvements to stay ahead of the competition.

When considering improvements to efficiency or performance of one's portfolio, the concept of risk versus reward is also an important factor. A race-car driver may decide that carrying less fuel makes the car lighter and therefore faster. But having to refuel at an inopportune time or risk breaking down altogether would be catastrophic to the outcome of a race. If Bryson swings too hard, he could lose control of the club and produce a problematic shot. Skiers who push themselves too hard could wipe out.

In all things, pushing the boundaries to obtain greater potential rewards involves an increasing degree of risk. But what could be risky behavior to an amateur on the way up might be foundational and easy for a seasoned professional. Thus, risk is a relative term, and it's important to balance one's tolerance for it against the potential rewards that taking it may produce.

Now that you have an idea of how much you need to save to confidently retire, it's important to examine how and where you're saving those dollars. Just like professional sports or any other competitive endeavor, you want to make sure you're using the resources you have as efficiently as possible and not wasting opportunities along the way. Additionally, you should be taking enough calculated risk to have the potential for gains over time, but not so much that a market downturn would cause you to panic and catastrophically derail your plans.

Too often, I have come across clients who are so fearful of losing money that they spend many years in savings vehicles or overly conservative investments with low yields, while opportunities for real wealth generation pass them by. With proper education and a plan that can withstand various market environments, one can feel the permission to stay more fully invested during tough times and maximize their long-term results. The combination of increasing efficiency through cost reduction and properly managing risk can be the difference between retiring on time or being forced to work several years longer.

ASSET ALLOCATION

One of the most important factors in investment management is how your assets are allocated across investment alternatives. Major asset classes include, but are not limited to, stocks, bonds, cash, real estate and commodities. Each of these asset classes have unique risk and return characteristics and may respond to various market environments differently.

Within these broad asset classes there are more specific classes of investments. Stocks may be defined as small, large or international, for example, and represent fractional ownership in a company. They are commonly traded on the open market, and their value will rise or fall as the perceived future value of the company increases or decreases. Shares of successful companies can appreciate quickly and generate extremely large returns for investors, while companies that fail can lead to complete loss of one's investment as the value of shares falls to zero.

Large, stable companies that produce valuable goods and services generally have lower risk of this kind of failure in the short run, and the prices of these stocks tend not to fluctuate as much as others. A lot of these companies also pay a dividend, meaning you receive a share of their profits each quarter as income. Smaller companies with a limited set of offerings, like a technology or pharmaceutical company, may appreciate much quicker as opportunities unfold, but also carry a much greater risk of going out of business.

It's common knowledge that the stock market is a great place to generate wealth over time. Stocks represent ownership in a company, and their value rises and falls with the expected earnings of that company over time. For most people, investing in a diversified fund that owns many stocks is how they gain exposure to the stock market. Over the last 96 years, the S&P 500, an index of the largest publicly traded stocks that is a proxy for "the stock market," has averaged a whopping 12.2% return—and that includes the Great Depression!

At that level of return, one could double their money roughly every six years. But with great reward comes great risk. While the best annual return for the stock market was 49% (in 1931), the worst year was -37% and occurred much more recently (in 2008). In fact, that worst year was closer to -50% if you measure from the height of the market in September 2007 to its bottom in March 2009.

Could you watch your portfolio lose half of its value and stay the course? To obtain that 12.2% average return, you would have had to do exactly that—something many investors are incapable of doing. According to DALBAR, the average individual investor underperforms the market by 1.81–4.13%, depending on the time period studied. This is because they tend to let emotion get the best of them in down years and sell their stocks to avoid any more pain.

But in all past market declines, stocks have recovered even more strongly, and those who sold stocks missed out on the biggest moves upward. Remember earlier when we discussed the cost of missing out on even 1% of your returns over time? Human emotion can be the costliest eroding factor in retirement income planning.

As you can see in Figure 2.1, stocks have produced outsized rewards over time. But that has generally been at the cost of higher price volatility, which is measured by something called *standard deviation*. Standard deviation is a statistical measure; it describes how much higher or lower than the average return an investment was about two-thirds of the time. The other third of the time, the returns were either higher or lower than that. This means that over the last 96 years, a pure stock portfolio returned 12.2% on average, and two-thirds of the time the annual returns were between -7.5% and 29.9%.

This may sound great to you, but those returns come at a cost—your emotions. Remember that the other third of the time, returns were either higher or lower than that range. In recent history, the S&P 500 lost almost half of its value twice; first with a three-year string of negative returns from 2000–2002 following the dot-com bubble, and then again in 2008 with the burst of the housing bubble. Could you keep your emotions in check and stay invested during a time like that?

Stock & Bond Portfolio Returns 1926–2021

Allocation (Stocks/Bonds)	0/100	20/80	40/60	60/40	80/20	100/0
Average Return	5.8%	7.1%	8.4%	9.7%	11.0%	12.3%
Loss Every __ Years	6.3	7.9	5.9	4.3	4.0	3.7
Worst Year	-5%	-10%	-19%	-27%	-35%	-43%

Figure 2.1: Stock/bond portfolios with various risk/return

Bonds have traditionally been the other major asset class for diversifying away from stocks. The common "60/40" portfolio refers to 60% allocated toward stocks and 40% allocated toward bonds. Bonds are issued by companies and governments as a way of borrowing money. They come in many forms, but the simplest bonds will pay you interest annually and then return your investment at the end of the term. For example, if you buy a typical 10-year, $1,000 bond that pays 5% interest, you would receive $50 per year for 10 years, then receive your full $1,000 back at the end of the 10-year term.

Bonds have two major risks. The first is default risk—the chance that the issuer (company or government) won't pay you back. For most investors buying bond *funds*, they needn't worry too much about one of the dozens or even hundreds of bond issuers defaulting. It would represent only a small percentage of the total portfolio. What many investors fail to realize, however, is that interest rate movements inversely impact what they can sell their bonds for.

This is the second, and more important, major risk. When interest rates rise, the value of your bonds go down, and vice versa. This is because, for example, if you purchased the bond mentioned above that pays 5% interest, but now other companies were issuing new bonds paying 10% interest, nobody would want to buy yours from you for what you paid ($1,000). Instead, they would pay you significantly less. On the other hand, if interest rates fall, the value of your bonds in the market would go up. This has been happening steadily since the early 1980s, as rates have consistently fallen for four decades. More on this in the next chapter.

DIVERSIFICATION

We've been taught not to put all of our eggs in one basket. While that basket may indeed be the best basket of all, it also means that any risks it is exposed to exposes *all* of our eggs to that risk. In investment planning, the term *diversification* refers to the practice of spreading our assets among numerous asset classes, so that if one does poorly, the others may perform differently or potentially even benefit from the conditions that caused the other to suffer. As such, this common strategy is not meant to generate outsized returns. Rather, it is meant to soften the blow of market downturns so investors can comfortably remain invested throughout all market environments. It is a mechanism that all responsibly constructed portfolios must employ to manage risk in order to invest for potential reward.

It's important to note that avoiding volatility isn't necessarily the goal of every investment portfolio. There are investors who have a very high tolerance for risk due to large pensions, guaranteed income, expected inheritance, the presence of other conservative assets in their portfolio or just due to a long time horizon until their retirement goal. But if large losses would either cause an investor to panic and sell low (thus locking in losses), or worse, derail retirement plans because those losses occurred too close to their retirement date, then risk mitigation through diversification is the common-sense approach.

Looking back at Figure 2.1, you can see that the more bonds you add into the mix, the less volatility (and average return) you historically realize. This is actually a good thing, because it makes the downswings a lot easier to stomach. The worst thing you can do is lose a lot of money (on paper) when the market goes down, panic and then sell your investments. This locks in losses and guarantees your portfolio won't recover, which it always would have after every historical downturn. The key is to take an acceptable amount of risk that you can tolerate even during the bad times so you're able to stay the course. Generally, the further you are from your goals, the more risk and stock market exposure you can take. As you approach your goals, there may not be enough time to fully recover from market downturns.

REBALANCING

Over time, the mix of your assets will shift as market forces make them either more valuable or less valuable. Furthermore, as you get closer to achieving your goals, you may wish to reduce the allocation to risky assets because you are less tolerant of large market losses. To ensure the risk/reward potential remains balanced and in line with your goals, you should examine and adjust your portfolio at least annually.

This means if your allocation toward stocks (which are also the most prone to large downswings) has increased due to positive market performance, you should take some of your gains off the table and use those proceeds to buy bonds or other assets according to your original asset mix. This practice has the desirable result of automatically selling assets that have performed well and buying assets that have underperformed at regular intervals. Buying low and selling high is the first principle of investing, and periodically rebalancing will help to ensure you remain diversified according to your goals while keeping your allocations from creeping up in riskiness due to market performance.

It's important you do this at regular intervals, and don't try to time the market. Waiting until your "gut" tells you it's time can leave your risk exposure in an inappropriate place. Timing the market has been proven impossible over and over. Your best bet is to employ ongoing techniques to capture returns according to a repeatable strategy.

DOLLAR COST AVERAGING

When should you make contributions to investment accounts? If you're thinking the market is expensive today because it's performed so well in recent history you'd be right, but what does that mean regarding the timing of your investments? Should you wait until the market has a downturn to make investments? Should you build up a large cash position and get ready to make that big investment when the time is right?

The reality is that timing that purchase just right is nearly impossible. The market is more nuanced than that, and volatility can be minimal for a very long period. So long, that you can watch incredible market returns continue to pass you by for many years without seeing a major market downturn or obvious opportunity to buy. A good example is the most recent decade or so. Since 2009, annual returns in the stock market were positive every year except for one. And that one bad year was very minor.

If you exercised what you felt to be caution, you would have missed out on your investments potentially quadrupling in value over that time with minimal fluctuation, save for a few months at the height of the pandemic. Rather than sitting on the sidelines, systematically investing small amounts over time can mitigate the risk of putting all of your money in the market right before a crash. Furthermore, when the market is down, your dollars buy more shares of an investment due to its depressed value.

By systematically buying into the market at regular intervals in the same amount, such as a monthly contribution, you can protect yourself against risking all of your money at once. Just like diversification, this practice hasn't historically generated outsize returns, but it provides one the comfort to invest by minimizing the downside potential. For younger investors with a longer time horizon, investing a lump sum all at once may still make the most sense.

ALTERNATE ASSETS

Traditional investments and asset classes are far from the only ways to accumulate substantial funds for retirement. Real estate has historically been among the most popular places to park wealth and obtain significant tax advantages.

In the most modest example, one can purchase a home early in their working years with a loan from a bank and make systematic payments toward that loan over the course of as many as 30 years. The leverage of these mortgage loans is what provides the potential to produce outsize returns in appreciating markets. Once those payments are finished, the investment becomes an appreciating asset in retirement. Through a reverse mortgage—or by downsizing and selling that home in exchange for a less expensive property—retirees can tap that equity. In other cases, a retiree may own one or more rental properties that can be used to supplement other investments and sources of income.

Gold, precious metals, art, collectibles, cryptocurrencies and NFTs all constitute other places one can store wealth and potentially gain when eventually selling them at greater value. These assets all have unique properties. Owning them is an attractive way for many investors to further diversify away from less tangible "paper" wealth. But just because one may be able to see, touch or interact with these assets, one should not view them as less risky. They each have their own risk profiles and costs of ownership associated with them to take into account. In general, as one moves up the wealth ladder and begins to maximize the tax advantages of traditional accounts, these alternatives become more attractive.

Insurance companies also offer a variety of extremely popular vehicles with incredible tax advantages, allowing one to accumulate wealth with upside potential while mitigating risks. Annuities, for example, have been around for centuries and allow one to trade a sum of money for guaranteed income that they can't outlive. This effectively turns a lifetime of savings into a pension. These vehicles also come in a variety of structures, some of which allow for a funding phase where one can accumulate wealth without taxation on the way up. Furthermore, they can often participate in stock or bond markets and offer guarantees about minimum rates of return or future income. I'll discuss these in greater depth in Chapter 6.

Similarly, permanent life insurance contracts allow one to accumulate cash values that can be accessed at various times throughout one's life. These contracts pay income tax-free death benefits and are one of the best-kept secrets in the financial-planning space, when structured properly. They can guarantee that money is left to loved ones while providing lifetime, unrestricted access to much of those funds for any purpose, whether it's retirement income, long-term care planning, emergency funds or anything else. These guarantees that are only offered by life insurance companies can be a key ingredient in one's permission to spend. They also have unique and very attractive tax advantages, but without many of the restrictions and rules of traditional retirement accounts. We'll discuss this further in Chapter 7.

When Steve and I met the next day, he arrived with his laptop ready to take action. We discussed how this one account was for retirement, and that his time horizon before actually touching that money was more than 10 years away. Furthermore, he had ample available savings, a steady career and a small pension available at work. Overall, his net worth had remained about flat over the quarter, meaning the rest of his finances were improving even though this one account was struggling. I reviewed a chart that looked like Figure 2.1 with him, and he remembered why he had invested this way. Greater risk and volatility have always been rewarded with greater upside. Steve's other savings and assets gave him permission to be more fully invested and to ride out short-term pain for long-term gain. Steve felt much better after that conversation and was delighted when his next quarterly statement showed most of those losses bouncing back, after the scary headlines had subsided.

Chapter 3
Taxes and Asset Location

Marika was so proud. When I got introduced to this young professional on the rise, she was quick to share how great a saver she was. Not only had she just about conquered her student loans, she was also saving over 15% of her income in her 401(k) and planned to save even more once her last loan payments were made. This woman had big goals. She wanted to buy real estate close to the city, start a family and eventually break away from her employer to start her own business. It was clear that she would become increasingly successful and wealthy over time, but was she saving money in the right way? Funding her plans at work was certainly easy, but she was concerned that it might not be the most efficient over time.

TAX TREATMENT OF ACCOUNTS

It's not how much you make, it's how much you keep, the old saying goes. Whether it's earned income from employment, income from investments, Social Security benefits or capital gains, the IRS will get its pound of flesh as your wealth increases. Understanding your options and where to put your money at various times throughout your life can have a major impact on how much money you have in retirement and what's left over *after taxes* for your loved ones as an inheritance. This is called *asset location*.

I described asset allocation—the major asset classes and types of investments one can engage with—in the previous chapter. But asset *location* refers to the accounts that hold those investments. Think of these accounts as wrappers for your investments. The government will tax you according to the rules of the wrapper, and they generally exist to allow for various methods of tax deferral. Obviously, taxation is a very broad and complex topic that goes beyond the scope of this book. But you should be aware of how your savings and investments are taxed so you can optimize how much you pay over time. The results can be dramatic.

For example, if you earn an 8% return on your investments but pay a 25% tax rate on your gains, you're really only *keeping* 6%, because 25% of 8% is 2%, and that's what the IRS gets. State and local governments are often entitled to a portion of those gains as well, making the net result even lower. So, when evaluating investment options and where to place them, thinking in terms of what's left over is the key.

In general, there are three major ways your investments are taxed: annually, tax-deferred or tax-free. And if your investment gains are taxed annually, those gains can be treated as either short-term or long-term, which can be a significant difference. Beyond that, there are endless considerations that business owners and high net-worth individuals should consult their tax professionals about, but for most individuals this general discussion will provide the bulk of what you need to know.

Tax-Deferred

People with earned income can contribute to individual retirement accounts (IRAs) and deduct up to $6,000 of those contributions from their taxable income each year (as of 2022). Savers aged 50 and older can save up to $7,000. The ability to exclude this from one's taxable income is a great benefit and incentive to save, particularly for individuals who pay high income tax rates. Those with qualified retirement plans at work, such as a 401(k), can save up to $20,500 per year, or $27,000 if they are over age 50. Business owners also have opportunities to contribute even more.

One of the most attractive features of 401(k) plans is that employers can offer a *match*, whereby they will match an employee's monthly payment to the plan as an incentive for workers to save. This matching contribution represents free money and immediate gain inside the plan, which should be attractive to any participant. For example, a common plan may offer a 100%, dollar-for-dollar match up to a 5% contribution. This means if an employee contributes $5,000 of her $100,000 salary, the company will contribute another $5,000 on her behalf. If she saved even more into the plan, the employer contributions would remain at only 5%.

Other plans may commonly offer a 50% match, perhaps up to a higher amount, like 6%. In such a case, the employee would save $6,000 of her own money and receive $3,000 from the employer. The bottom line is that this is an immediate 50% or 100% gain on the contribution, and no argument about fees or taxation can convince me that that's a bad thing. However, contributions over and above the company match may be more effectively invested elsewhere.

These types of plans generally come with strings attached, dictating when money *may* be taken out (usually after age 59½) without penalty taxes, and when one must begin taking *required* minimum distributions. Congress has provided this beneficial tax treatment to help people save for retirement, which is why there are strict rules involved. If you take distributions from the account prior to age 59½, not only are taxes due on the entire distribution, but you must pay an extra 10% penalty for what's viewed as an early withdrawal. When considering the spirit of the tax advantage, it is to encourage the average working American to save their own money toward their future (and not be reliant on Social Security or government assistance).

In the event you're successful enough to retire young or simply choose to cash out and invest elsewhere, the IRS will collect its taxes and a bit extra. This is a very strong incentive to keep your retirement plans intact. Similarly, if you've had other successes or accumulated too much money, the IRS will not allow you to defer taxation indefinitely. Distributions must begin by age 72 so the IRS can begin collecting taxes on the money. Required distributions begin somewhat small, at about 3.7% of the account balance at age 72. However, the required percentage rises to 8.2% of the account by age 90, and those living to age 100 will be required to take 15.6% of the account out that year. For successful savers, these requirements on top of other income sources in retirement can push them into unfavorably high income tax brackets.

Tax-Free

IRAs and 401(k) plans can be characterized as "Roth," which reverses the tax treatment. Instead of getting a tax deduction up front, individuals make contributions after tax, but all future growth and gains come out income tax-free. This can be a tremendous benefit, particularly for pre-retirees who are in lower income tax brackets or expect their taxes to rise over time. Contribution limits for Roth IRAs or 401(k) plans are the same as traditional accounts. But individual retirement accounts come with the added limitation that in 2022 one's income must be below $144,000, or $214,000 if married and filing jointly. Once again, these benefits were put in place to allow the common American the ability to save for retirement and enjoy favorable tax treatment as a reward. High income earners aren't viewed as needing advantages or incentives to accumulate wealth.

Permanent life insurance policies also receive similar beneficial tax treatment, with death benefits payable income tax-free. Unlike term life insurance—which is inexpensive temporary coverage that the insurer doesn't expect to pay claims on—permanent life insurance has an inevitable gain. It pays out *when* you die, not *if* you die. The IRS generally allows these death benefits, which may greatly exceed the sum of all premiums paid, to be paid income tax-free. This is a tremendous advantage for those who expect to leave significant assets to their children, church or charitable interests upon death. Many types of plans also allow for the tax-deferred buildup of cash value that is accessible at any time without the strict limitations imposed on retirement accounts. Additionally, through special loan provisions that are unique to this type of vehicle, one can generally access gains without being taxed. This access to capital without taxation or pre-59½ penalties like you'd have with a retirement account make them very attractive.

These tax advantages come with few limitations, and the contractual guarantees make them one of the best-kept secrets in the business. They have been a favorite tool of well-educated investors for a very long time. The catch is that one must be healthy enough to qualify (it is life insurance, after all).

Taxed Annually

Investments don't need to be owned in retirement accounts or any other "wrapper." In fact, there may be good reasons to hold them outside. Interest-bearing accounts like savings accounts, money market funds, bonds, or investments sold for a profit within one year will generally add to one's earned income that year. That income will be taxed at that person's individual tax bracket; in some cases, it may push them into a higher marginal tax bracket. For investors with low current income, this may be more favorable than deferring taxation until a later date when total income may be higher.

Certain investments sold for a gain after one year, such as common stock in a company, may be taxed at a special (lower) long-term capital gains rate. This is how many wealthy people pay low taxes. Much of their wealth and income is derived from ownership in firms rather than employment. During a recent election cycle, Warren Buffett (one of the richest people in the world), was famously quoted as saying his administrative assistant pays a higher tax rate than him. This is because his income comes from selling appreciated stock at much lower long-term capital gains rates, rather than traditional income tax rates.

As I hope you're beginning to see, strategically beginning with the end in mind and having a retirement distribution strategy well before you get there can inform how you position yourself to minimize taxes over time.

THE BIG TAX MISTAKE

Nobody likes paying taxes. The government has provided several beneficial ways to defer taxation, but blindly kicking the can down the road can lead to a tax time bomb that's impossible to defuse. Think of it like routine maintenance on your car. Paying for service along the way can help you avoid more costly or even catastrophic repairs later. The same applies to the taxation of your investments. By deferring taxes, you're essentially creating a growing debt to the IRS, and you can't predict the tax rates of the future.

For most investors, their 401(k) or retirement account is their largest asset outside of their primary residence. That 401(k) was most likely funded with tax-deferred dollars, meaning that withdrawals in retirement will be fully taxable. Conventional wisdom on the matter generally says that if you expect to be in a lower tax bracket in retirement, then deferral is a good thing—much more favorable than paying taxes at younger ages. Conversely, if you believe your tax rates will be higher in the future, you should choose a tax-free or Roth option, paying taxes now and letting your investments compound. So, what do you do?

You cannot know what your tax rate will be in retirement. Politicians of the future will have the power to change rates, and your portfolio will change dramatically over time as markets shift, career paths diverge and life unfolds. What you *can* do is diversify, so when it's time to take income, you have choices. By having a significant portion of your retirement assets in a tax-free source, you gain control over how much you pay each year. Keep in mind that pension income, company matches, Social Security income or other deferred company benefits are generally all taxable in retirement. Required minimum distributions from your retirement plans will force you to start recognizing additional income no matter what. As discussed earlier, these could combine to put you in higher and higher tax brackets.

When you die, whatever is left in your traditional (tax-deferred) retirement accounts is subject to income tax based on the size of the account. This means that if you die with $1 million in the account, it will be taxed like an individual earning an ordinary income of $1 million that year. If there is a surviving spouse, it can be rolled into their individual retirement account without current taxation, but the same rules will apply upon their passing.

Until recently, there was also a popular provision that allowed for a plan called a "stretch IRA," whereby children of the deceased retiree could *stretch* distributions of their inherited IRA account over the course of their own life expectancies. This allowed them to spread income, and therefore taxes, over time. But with the passage of the SECURE Act in 2019, inherited retirement accounts must now be fully withdrawn within 10 years. At normal life expectancies for the retiree (80–90 years old in many cases), adult children inheriting these accounts are likely to be in their peak income-earning years, and these distributions can often push them into the highest tax brackets. These new rules have the potential to make the "wait and see" approach of the past wildly ineffi-cient. Put differently, after your death, your beneficiaries and the government will each take a share of your savings and investments. By being proactive and planning ahead, you can minimize what goes to the government and maximize what stays in the family.

THE FUTURE OF INCOME TAXES

Financial pundits have traditionally parroted that there's no way to know what future taxes will be, so you might as well defer until later. On top of that, they assert that you'll need less income in retirement, so your tax rates will be lower. But not so fast. As we discussed in Chapter 1, if you've done relatively well and plan to enjoy life to the fullest in retirement, it's very possible you'll need the same amount of income or potentially even more. And while income may be higher, it's worth considering what could cause politicians to push income tax rates higher.

First, we are in a historically low interest rate environment due to the Tax Cuts and Jobs Act of 2017. This act, signed into law by President Trump, lacked the bipartisan support to make it permanent. Instead, it provided for lower income tax rates enacted to last only eight years, through the 2025 tax year. In 2026, federal income tax brackets are set to revert back to what they were in 2017, with appropriate adjustments for inflation.

Since that time, however, a Democrat has been elected to the White House, and control of Congress has been split, making permanent tax changes unlikely. Therefore, many Americans, particularly married couples earning six-figure combined incomes, will see significant tax increases. This is currently legislated to happen; Congress needn't do anything to raise taxes going forward. For the next few years, taxes are "on sale"—meaning you're almost certainly paying less tax on the same income today than you will in just a few years. If you can pay taxes today and invest it someplace where it won't be taxed again, that is a good deal.

Second, tax rates were low already. Since the early 1980s, federal income tax rates in America have generally been falling for all but the top 20% of earners. Additionally, except for a handful of years around 1990, top marginal tax brackets for the wealthiest Americans have been the lowest since almost a century ago. This is important because the reason for this shift is the widening wealth gap in America. The wealthy are getting wealthier, and the gap between the economic classes is growing larger. Increasingly, the wealthy have all the money. Regardless of one's politics, math alone can tell you that if the government needs to raise revenue, it has to come from the people who actually have income or wealth to tax. As your success—or diligent investing—propels you up the economic ladder, you will simultaneously be making yourself a bigger tax target.

Finally, have you seen the national debt? At the time of this writing, it sat at over $31 trillion, or around $247,000 per taxpayer. (Check the U.S. Debt Clock for current numbers.) This amount of debt is unsustainable without a major economic boom on the horizon. Economists generally speak of the national debt in terms of the ratio between debt and GDP (Gross Domestic Product, the measure of all goods and services produced in the U.S.). This ratio describes debt in relation to the overall economy. It's a way to adjust for inflation and gauge how bad things really are. To put it in perspective, the country has only had higher debts relative to the total economy once, and that was at the height of World War II. Following the war, the economy took off. That growth eclipsed the debt while also providing opportunities for the government to collect taxes and pay it down. Whether that will occur again is anyone's guess. There is a growing number of economists who subscribe to "modern monetary theory." It asserts that things are different this time and we needn't worry about rising national debts. But common sense and historical precedent suggest otherwise. Regardless of what's to come, we are most certainly not facing a political and economic environment that will favor tax cuts for those with wealth in America.

Because of all this, you simply *must* add tax-free sources of income to your retirement portfolio. If you qualify for Roth contributions, that's a great way to avoid future taxation while participating in the traditional major asset classes. Permanent life insurance is another great way to save, avoiding future taxation while maintaining complete access to your money before retirement. Many of the wealthiest Americans use it to great financial advantage. It's among the most misunderstood tax strategies available to the common investor. Owning your own business or real estate are other great ways to grow your wealth while obtaining significant tax advantages. In the end, it's all about diversification. In the last chapter we talked about diversifying across asset classes (asset allocation), and in this chapter we talked about diversifying across tax treatments (asset location). When the time comes to spend down or pass on your lifetime of savings, this puts you in maximum control.

Marika was doing a great thing by saving so much, but she was doing so without any strategy for the future. Not only was she likely to be in a higher tax bracket in years to come (and probably the rest of her life), but she was going to need access to that money along the way. By reallocating those dollars toward tax-free accounts like a Roth IRA and permanent life insurance, she reduced her total tax exposure over time, lowered her risk, provided for loved ones and obtained access to those funds along the way without any age restrictions. For Marika, it wasn't about how much she was saving but rather where she was putting it.

Chapter 4
Risks to Your Retirement

He was a millionaire who had just retired from a successful career as an architect. With a solid seven-figure retirement account balance (in addition to other assets), it was clear that Gary needn't worry about making ends meet for the rest of his life. Yet, when asked what he wanted to do in retirement, he seemed paralyzed. He wanted to travel internationally, play golf at nice courses, drive a Mercedes and take his grandchildren on vacation. During his working years he did all of those things without worry, because the next paycheck was always on the way. However, now that the paychecks had stopped and he needed to make his nest egg last the rest of his life, those large expenses became scary. How could he know if he was spending too much? Would that lifestyle jeopardize his accounts? What if he needed to withdraw even more for unforeseen events? What would happen if he ran out of money?

Planning to spend down your money is theoretically very simple if you can predict the future, but all the potential "what ifs" keep people clutching their cash. These risks can be defined as anything that threatens the assumptions we made when determining how much we need to have saved for retirement. A risk to your retirement plan is therefore any occurrence that is worse than assumed. It's crazy to list all the little eventualities that can occur in retirement. A more realistic approach is to remain somewhat flexible and have plans in place that allow you to adapt to whatever the world throws at you. People don't lose sleep over what they can control. Maintaining control in the face of unexpected events is what your permission-to-spend plan is all about.

Risks can be lumped into three overarching categories, which I call the three Es of retirement risk: economic risk (sequence of returns, inflation, interest rates and so on); expense risk (potential to need large lump sums or significantly more income, usually for health care); and endurance risk. These categories matter because they may cause us to require more money at a time when we are increasingly incapable of working to earn income. Fear of these unlikely but very possible outcomes can cause retirees to hold back on spending *just in case* bad things happen, leading to a tragic under-enjoyment of retirement in the vast majority of cases. Therefore, we need to understand the risks and plan for them in advance to obtain permission to spend.

ECONOMIC RISK

It might make sense for some to think of their retirement portfolio as a business. A viable business, by its simplest definition, is something that generates cash flows that exceed expenses. In retirement, you generally have a combination of income from investments, Social Security and pensions. To have a viable retirement, your sources of income must comfortably exceed planned expenses—and be expected to do so for decades to come. Market forces that affect the value of the income from those sources can be viewed as economic risks to your retirement.

In Chapter 2, I discussed the importance of having risk in your pre-retirement portfolio; over time, that risk will reward investors with outsize returns. This is also important when in retirement, but one must be more diversified and have a strategy for taking income from alternate sources when markets falter. Being forced to sell investments when they are down locks in losses and makes it impossible to recover. In terms of dollar cost averaging, market volatility actually helps because our systematic purchases are made at lower stock prices during market downturns.

The problem in retirement is that dollar cost averaging on the way out works in reverse. When the market is down, you must sell more shares to obtain the same income. The remainder of the portfolio then needs even higher gains to return to previous levels. This is also referred to as *sequence of returns risk*, which we will discuss in depth in the next chapter. In short, diversification becomes far more important in retirement. A successful retiree should have multiple sources of income so they aren't forced to sell anything when its value is down.

Interest rates are extremely important for retirees as well, since they are what drive the earnings on their savings accounts. Since retirees are less risk-tolerant, they tend to have more money in cash and fixed-income investments. In the past, retirees could invest in Certificates of Deposit (CDs) or bonds and live off the interest, keeping the principal intact and rolling it over at the end when the investments matured. Now, with interest rates so low, retirees are forced to seek returns in assets that bear greater risks. If interest rates rise, that may seem like a win for retirees, but as mentioned before, rising interest rates may cause bond funds—the traditional alternative to stock market investments—to suffer.

EXPENSE RISK

Inflation is another market force that is significantly rearing its ugly head for the first time in almost 40 years. Inflation refers to the cost of goods and services in the economy. When the cost of things rises, the same amount of dollars buys less of those things. In general, this needn't be a huge problem if your income is rising in tandem, but it can put a lot of pressure on a retirement portfolio.

Inflation-adjusted income (discussed at the beginning of this book and in greater detail in the next chapter) is important for retirees of modest means, who have a lesser ability to reduce spending if needed. Wealthier retirees who can cut back on lifestyle will be better able to weather inflationary storms. Exposure to the stock market has proven to be a great way to protect one's portfolio from inflation. But pension income is generally not inflation-adjusted and can therefore be a problem for retirees with a fixed income in an inflationary environment.

Large expenses can also derail an otherwise sound retirement strategy. The most noteworthy of these expenses is long-term care, which is defined as chronic, ongoing care that generally isn't covered by any medical plan. Medicare and other health plans are there to cover the treatment of various conditions. However, they are not designed to cover the cost of aides and other ongoing support for the activities of daily living.

Long-term care insurance has also been around for decades. It protects against the potentially high cost of ongoing care (typically at advanced ages) that isn't covered by traditional medical coverage or Medicare. Those programs are designed to cover the cost to treat conditions with the expectation of recovery. Long-term care generally is described as assistance with two out of six "activities of daily living," such as bathing, dressing, eating, transferring, toileting and continence. Additionally, cognitive disorders such as dementia or Alzheimer's disease can cause one to need assistance. The options for care range from occasional home care to assisted living facilities with graduating levels of dependence to a full skilled-care nursing facility.

As you'd expect, costs rise as one moves across this spectrum, with national average costs exceeding $100,000 per year for private room care. If you live in certain areas of the country, such as wealthy areas like the NYC suburbs, your costs could easily be double what you'd pay elsewhere. With all of that said, the likelihood that you will require care is quite high. Roughly 50% of the population will require long-term care at some point in their lifetime. About half of those who need care will only require it for a couple of years or less, typically right before they die. This is generally not what we are worried about in terms of financial planning because the expenses are temporary and not likely to wipe out a retirement portfolio. The real risk is when ongoing care lasts several years or longer, and existing sources of income or assets aren't enough to cover the costs.

No family wants to see their loved ones suffer. They'll typically do anything within their power to pay for care for as long as necessary, even if that means financial ruin. With scarce resources, sometimes adult children will leave the workforce or work part-time so they can care for aging parents, much like they do when they have children. No parent wants to be a burden on their children in this way. More importantly, no retiree wants to be forced into a limited set of difficult choices due to improper planning or a failure to perceive potential risk.

Having access to additional resources through insurance not only mitigates the financial risk, but also puts the retiree in greater control of how and where they'll receive care. In fact, most available policies provide for a care coordination benefit to help the family at the time of a claim.

ENDURANCE RISK

Also known as longevity risk, this is a multiplier of other risks because they become more likely to occur the longer you are alive. Living a long time means your portfolio must last longer and weather more economic storms. It also increases the potential that you'll undergo a period of time that requires expensive long-term care. Guaranteed income from pensions, Social Security or annuities helps one know that no matter how long they live, there will be a reliable flow of money coming in. Understanding and maximizing these sources of income is crucial to granting yourself permission to spend. We will cover this in greater detail in Chapter 6.

Many retirees tend to underestimate how long they need to plan for. Their parents and grandparents often died in their 70s and 80s, so it's hard to envision living much longer than that. However, people are living longer today than in the past, and diseases that used to be death sentences are often manageable with modern medicine. As you can see in Figure 4.1, a pair of healthy 65-year-olds have a 50% chance that at least one of them will still be alive at age 90. Planning for a retirement that could last 40 years is something you must seriously consider.

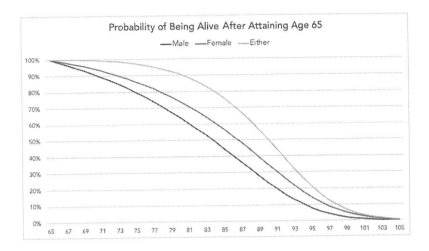

Figure 4.1: Survival probability for a 65-year-old couple

BEING MINDFUL OF MARKETS

Most educated investors know they shouldn't try to time the markets. This means you shouldn't wait to buy stocks until they look cheap, nor should you sell them when they look high. In fact, you shouldn't try to make any calls at all; you should simply choose an allocation with appropriate risk, spread your money across accounts with different tax treatment, make regular contributions and stay the course. And the longer your time horizon before needing to take income from that portfolio, the truer that is.

However, we are living in a time of extremes. Stock market valuations are at levels rarely seen before, and interest rates are lower than ever. In Figure 4.2, you can see the CAPE (cyclically adjusted price to earnings) ratio as of the beginning of 2022. CAPE is a metric invented and popularized by Nobel laureate Robert J. Shiller. It takes the current price of the stock market and compares it to the last 10 years of inflation-adjusted earnings to get a relative view of how expensive the market is versus what companies actually produced.

At the time of writing, it had come down from where it started in 2022, but one can clearly see that the last time it was that high was the peak of the dot-com bubble. Going back almost 100 years, that peak was the end of the Roaring Twenties, right before the Great Depression. This metric is actually not a great predictor of what's to come *next* year, so don't take this to mean that I'm predicting a stock market crash in the near term. However, it has proven to be a great predictor of what's to come over the next 10 years. We don't want to attempt to time the markets, but if you're approaching your goal of retirement, it might make sense to take some risk off the table or just make new contributions elsewhere.

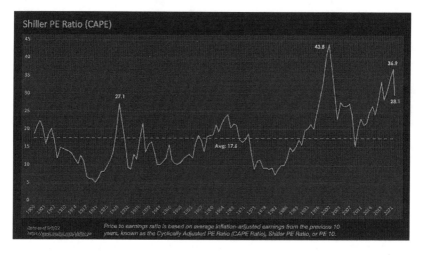

Figure 4.2: Shiller PE Ratio (CAPE)

Speaking of extremes, our persistently low interest rate environment has completely changed the outlook for the more conservative portion of our portfolios, such as bonds and cash. Savings accounts earn almost nothing right now, but the more important issue is what this has done to bond investments. Generally speaking, you earn money on bonds in two ways. The first is through the interest payment on the bond, also known as the coupon payment. Bonds will pay this annual rate until maturity, the time at which the investor's money (their principal) is returned.

The other way to make money in bonds is through capital appreciation (discussed in Chapter 2). As interest rates fall, new bond issues become less valuable than those issued in the past that paid higher interest. Because of this, you can sell your bonds to new investors who will pay you *more* for your bond than you paid for it.

In Figure 4.3, you can see how interest rates have changed over the last 150 years. Since rates peaked in 1981, we've experienced the biggest bull market for bonds ever, due to interest rates continuing to fall steadily. The average long-term corporate bond investor earned more than a 10% return over that period of time, and only suffered seven losing years out of 40—all relatively minor. What's most interesting about this chart is when you go back over the exact same period of time that ended in 1981. It started in 1942, the last time the rate environment was this low. Even though the rate environment is nearly a mirror image—because the direction of rates was *up* instead of *down*—returns were under 3%, with negative returns almost a quarter of the time. Thus, in an environment of rising interest rates, bonds almost certainly will not be the great diversifier that they have been in the recent past.

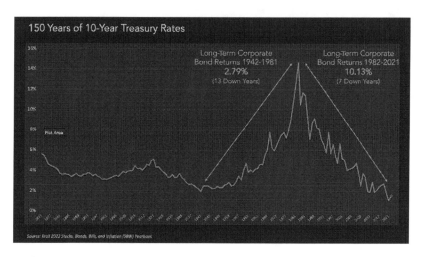

Figure 4.3: 150 Years of 10-Year Treasury Rates & Bond Performance

And in case that's not convincing enough, check out Figure 4.4 below, the chart of annual bond returns dating back almost 100 years. The 10-year U.S. treasury rate is also included in the chart to demonstrate the movement of interest rates over that same period of time. Almost every time you see bonds lose value, there is a corresponding peak in interest rates. At the time of this writing, the sharp move upward in rates in 2022 is setting bonds up for their worst year on record.

Conversely, almost every time you see bond returns soar, there is a downward move in interest rates that year. Most importantly, you can see how abnormal the last several decades have been. Unlike the stock market, the bond market is purely based on math. We have been at a mathematical peak in the bond market, and rates would need to rise quite a bit from here to support returns like those we've seen in the past. And if that occurs, there will be a lot of volatility and pain in the bond market on the way up.

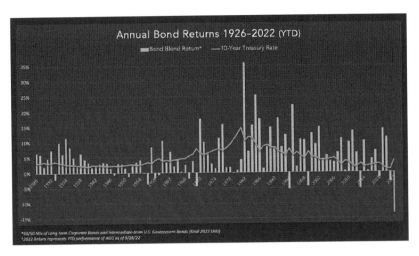

Figure 4.4: Bond Returns vs. 10-Year Treasury Rates since 1926

There's no way to predict which way interest rates will move, but in theory, they cannot go much lower over time. Rates are already historically low, and while rates have been negative elsewhere in the world, there is a limit to how much investors will tolerate this. Think about it—with negative interest rates, you're paying the bank to hold your money!

There comes a point when it's cheaper to just build your own bank, which creates that theoretical lower bound. In the short run, we could certainly experience a period where rates go lower and therefore help bonds. But over the course of decades, interest rates can really only stay low or rise. In a persistently low interest rate environment, both bonds and cash suffer. But in a rising interest rate environment, not only will bonds not produce great returns, but volatility and the potential for loss is greatly magnified—as we saw in the middle of the last century.

What could cause interest rates to rise? Inflation.

Since the 1970s, the Federal Reserve (the Fed) has been focused on following through on its dual mandate of achieving full employment and price stability. In the 1970s, the U.S. economy suffered through stagflation; the economy's growth was anemic while prices rose dramatically. In economic theory, inflation is described as money chasing a scarce amount of goods. Think of it as people collectively bidding prices up. If businesses raise prices and demand doesn't fall, this leads to inflation.

The Fed attempts to fight inflation through raising interest rates. High interest rates make saving attractive. People decide to save and invest their money instead of spending it. In 1981, the Fed raised rates to never-before-seen heights to stave off inflation, which kicked off that large bull market in bonds I described earlier in this chapter. It also stopped inflation in its tracks. In Figure 4.5 below, you can see how, as inflation trailed off over the following decades, so interest rates fell. In 2021, the United States saw significant inflation for the first time in many years. As of late 2022, the Fed had already increased interest rates and signaled that they're prepared to fight it as they have in the past.

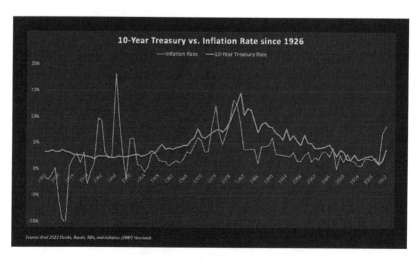

Figure 4.5: 10-Year Treasury vs. Inflation Rate since 1926

Putting this all together, if stock and bond markets look riskier than ever, and you can't hide in cash because it's earning so little, then what is an investor to do? Trying to time the markets and guess what the future holds is certainly not the answer. Countless fortunes have been lost and many opportunities have been missed trying to do exactly that.

But what if there were alternate assets one could add to their portfolio that would provide predictable growth while not risking exposure to these short-term market risks? Having an asset like this would grant that investor permission to remain fully invested in their diversified portfolio, knowing they have money available and won't be forced to sell low to generate income to live. It's time to take a deeper look at retirement income planning and putting a bulletproof strategy in place to weather any storm.

Gary was afraid to spend because he feared he might eventually run out of money. Through a thoughtful discussion of what could go wrong, we identified the major risks that could derail his retirement. Identifying and quantifying those risks were the first steps toward the financial freedom and worry-free retirement Gary was seeking. In subsequent meetings, we put plans and guarantees in place that would put Gary in control of worst-case outcomes, giving him permission to spend and enjoy the fruits of his lifetime of labor.

Chapter 5
Safe Withdrawal Rates and Sequence of Returns Risk

Gary's fear about his rate of spending came from reading about something called the 4% rule of retirement. This "rule" suggested that, historically speaking, one could take no more than 4% as an initial withdrawal rate from their retirement portfolio without risking that the portfolio wouldn't last as long as their retirement. Nobody wants to outlive their money or face the prospect of being bankrupt in their 90s. Even though Gary had saved quite a bit and arrived at retirement with ample savings, 4% of his investments didn't quite fund the lifestyle he wanted. He didn't want to overspend, but he was frustrated because life could also be very short. How could he freely spend his assets if he had to make sure they lasted as long as him?

I wrote this book because clients are being dramatically under-served by the financial services industry. It does a great job giving advice and education to pre-retirees on how to live below their means, save diligently, invest in financial products and plan for the future. It promises that if they do this throughout their 40-year working career, they will one day reach the promised land called retirement.

This advice is all good, but too often it stops there and falls way short. This is because when the retiree gets there and returns to the financial advisor to ask how much they can spend, the advisor's answer is often pathetic. That advisor may say, "Well, we're not really sure how long you're going to live. We're not sure what the market is going to do, and we're not sure if you're going to have expensive health-care concerns. Not to mention, there could be wars, pandemics, or major depressions in the market. We suggest you live below your means, hold back and base spending on the worst-case scenario. And if it turns out later in your life that we didn't need to be so conservative, we can increase your income then."

That's not a plan. That's not permission to spend. That's being reactive and operating based on fear because the only focus was on accumulating assets, without any proactive strategy for how to spend those assets. In my opinion, that's malpractice if the advisor's job is to help their client make decisions early in life that enable maximum enjoyment and financial value.

Retirement income planning is actually a pretty new field. Historically, workers would go to work for a company that offered a pension in return for years of service. It was up to the company to make investments on behalf of the worker to ensure they could fund those promised benefits. Social Security would eventually help, and a retiree may have other modest savings as well. If the mortgage was paid off by retirement, that could be enough.

In the 1980s, the country began shifting from defined benefit (pension) plans toward defined contribution (401(k)) plans. Employee contributions to the plan shifted the burden for retirement saving to the employee. Employers tradition-ally offer matching contributions, which is generally far less expensive than providing a pension. But even with that shift, retirement planning wasn't historically all that difficult. When one could actually get reasonably high interest rates on CDs, savings bonds and money market funds, retirees could invest their retirement funds in conservative vehicles and live off the interest. So long as they did not invade their principal, they were generally expected to be alright.

When rates began to fall below levels that would provide acceptable conservative investment income in retirement, some advisors began to study whether it might be prudent to take systematic income out of volatile investment portfo-lios, regardless of the interest rates or the returns they were earning. In 1994, an advisor by the name of William Bengen published his seminal study, which led to what has become commonly known as the "4% rule" of retirement income. Using stock, bond and inflation data that began in 1926, Bengen sought to determine what the maximum sustainable starting withdrawal rate was for each year, assuming retirement lasted 30 years. He dubbed this rate the SAFEMAX. It represents the highest amount one could draw from a portfolio in their first year, after which they would adjust withdrawals for inflation.

The hypothetical investment portfolio comprised 50% stocks and 50% bonds. It was rebalanced at the end of each year to keep the allocation constant. The results varied quite a bit year to year, but the worst scenario, which was a retirement beginning in 1966, showed a SAFEMAX rate of just over 4%. Therefore, historically speaking, so long as you started with income that represented no more than 4% of your starting balance, you could increase it each year at the actual inflation rate and still have money left in all scenarios.

You would never have to worry where interest rates were or what markets were doing.

Bengen's study was never meant to imply that 4% or any other number should be viewed as *safe*, or tell present-day retirees what to do. But the elegance and simplicity of the 4% rule quickly took hold as a starting point and foundational assumption in the budding field of retirement income planning.

Since then, countless iterations of Bengen's research have been conducted to look at different investment portfolios, inflation assumptions, retirement durations, inclusion of fees and the like. My own research in Figure 5.1 below shows similar results, with key differences being a 60/40 stock/bond allocation and the inclusion of common investment fees, which an investor would pay in real life. What stands out is how different the results were when applied to various periods of time.

The problem with retiring in the 1960s is that it was right before a period of very high inflation, poor bond returns due to rising rates and a stock market that was stagnant. Assuming the need for inflation-adjusted income meant increased stress on the portfolio with ever-increasing income being pulled from it. The result was a safe withdrawal rate of only about 3.5%, or $35,000 of income in a million-dollar portfolio. It's hard to feel like a millionaire when living off less than $100 per day. On the other hand, a retiree in 1982—at the beginning of the biggest bond bull market ever, when inflation was also decreasing and the stock market was strong—could have had *triple* the safe starting income of the 1960s retiree.

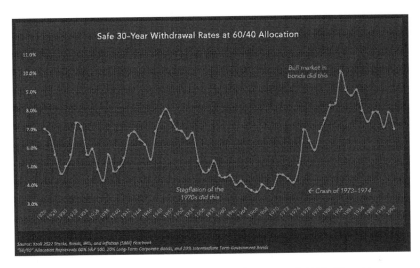

Figure. 5.1: Safe 30-Year Initial Withdrawal Rates at 60/40 Allocation

While this is all fun to talk about, an investor facing retirement has no clue what their scenario will end up looking like. History can only serve as a general guide of where to start, and each investor needs to check and adjust their spending at least annually to ensure they remain on track. That said, understanding what caused the negative scenarios to be so stark is the key to developing a strategy that can maximize retirement income in a way that can weather any financial storm. Thinking in terms of probability, Figure 5.2 is a representation of how often a given initial withdrawal rate would have been successful. Again, success is defined as still having money left in the retirement account at the end of 30 years.

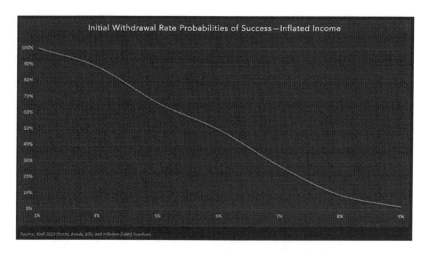

Figure 5.2: Initial Withdrawal Rate Probabilities of Success—
Inflated *Income*

A REALISTIC APPROACH TO INFLATION

Recall that one of the main reasons for the safe withdrawal rates of the 1960s was the high inflation that accelerated during the 1970s. But what if, as discussed before, an affluent retiree who naturally decreased discretionary spending over time didn't have the need for inflation-adjusted income? Instead, they could start their income much higher, keeping it relatively level as inflation gradually ate away at purchasing power and their appetite for purchasing similarly waned.

What impact would that have had on safe withdrawal rates? As you can see in my research in Figure 5.3, the impact is dramatic, with safe withdrawal rates increasing by 2–3% on average. That translates to *much* higher initial withdrawal rates at a time in retirement that the retiree is most likely to be able to enjoy that income to its fullest potential. As you'll note, the SAFEMAX withdrawal rate is still somewhat low but the lowest safe withdrawal rate has shifted from 1966 to 1929 with level income. This was the Great Depression era. So, assuming we don't repeat the Great Depression, major improvements could be made to retirement income for more affluent clients who are more able and willing to make necessary adjustments to their spending along the way.

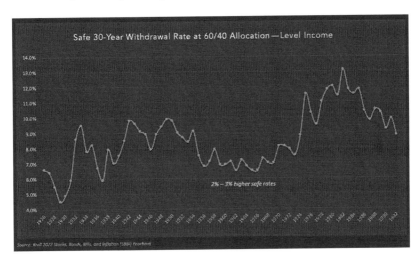

*Figure 5.3: Safe 30-Year Withdrawal Rate with **Level** Income*

Viewed in terms of probability of success, like before, one can see that almost a 6.5% initial withdrawal rate with level income provides a similar probability of success as 4% with level income.

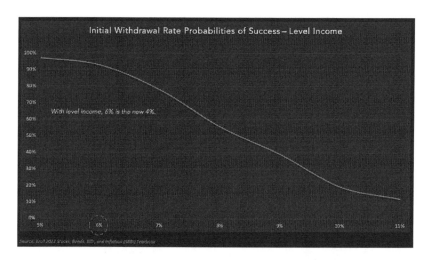

Figure. 5.4: Initial Withdrawal Rate Probabilities of Success—
Level *Income*

A large body of research demonstrates that retirees tend to spend less over time. The degree to which spending declines depends largely on income levels, with more affluent retirees realizing greater declines over time as discretionary spending goes down. To provide some perspective on the numbers in Figure 5.4, you can see in Figure 5.5 how much lifestyle one would be forfeiting by inaccurately assuming they need inflation-adjusted income. In two scenarios with similar historical probabilities of success (4% inflated vs. 6.5% level), it takes 18 years at 3% inflation for annual income to catch up to what one would have from a level source. In periods of high inflation this crossover would occur earlier, but in most historical cases it would not.

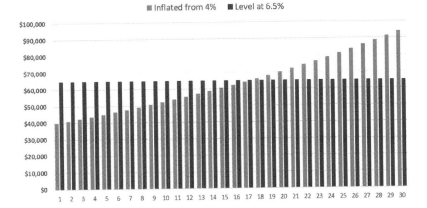

Figure 5.5: Annual Income—Inflation Adjusted vs. Level
($1M Starting Balance, 3% Inflation)

Taking this discussion a step further and looking at cumulative income, the inflation-adjusted scenario takes more than 30 years to catch up. This is what I'm referring to when I say that the financial services industry is grossly under-serving its retired clients, because too often the advice is to play it safe and operate from a place of fear. Managing client incomes based on the worst cases that history has provided means that in that vast majority of real-life outcomes, the retiree would have been drastically under-enjoying the retirement they spent decades working toward.

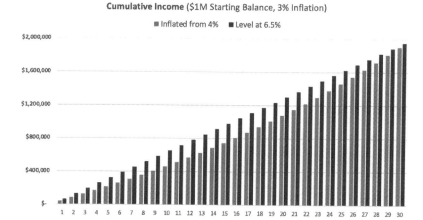

Figure 5.6: Cumulative Income ($1M Starting Balance, 3% Inflation)

Still not sold on the lack of need for inflation-protected income from your portfolio? Don't forget that almost all retirees will also enjoy income from Social Security. Social Security is an inflation-adjusted income source that can help mitigate the risk of high inflation in retirement, particularly for those who elect to delay benefits until their later years. Furthermore, deferred income annuities or qualified longevity annuity contracts (QLACs) can also mitigate the risk. I'll discuss both in depth in the next chapter.

Whether you started low and took inflated income or started high to keep it level, there was an additional force that factored into the wildly different safe withdrawal rates of the past. This force was *sequence of returns risk*. It is one of the most important factors in the sustainability of one's retirement portfolio.

SEQUENCE OF RETURNS RISK

In retirement, staying the course may not always be possible because of the need for income. If your primary source of income is your investment portfolio and the market goes down, you have no choice but to sell a portion of your portfolio low and effectively make that year's negative return even worse. Furthermore, when your portfolio has a depressed value, the same level of income now represents a greater percentage of it, exacerbating the issue. It can be quite difficult to recover from this. For this reason, average returns in retirement don't matter as much as the *sequence of returns*. To illustrate, consider the following example. Over the last 22 years, even with two of the largest stock market declines in history, aggressive investors with a hypothetical 80/20 portfolio experienced an average annual return of 8.54%.

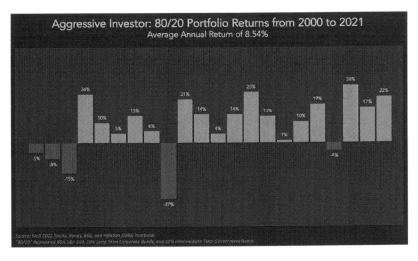

Figure 5.7: Hypothetical 80/20 portfolio annual returns (2000–2021)

If one considers taking a 6% initial withdrawal rate during a period that averaged 8.54%, they might assume that they would be safe and would still be making money during that period. However, experiencing negative returns early in that period and then compounding those losses by taking income would create an even worse environment that would become impossible to dig out of. Even though the latter half of this return pattern was historically strong, it was too little too late. In the example in Figure 5.8, a retiree starting with $2 million and withdrawing $120,000 per year would be left with only $159,593. This retiree, likely in their 80s at that point, would be one market crash away from running out of money.

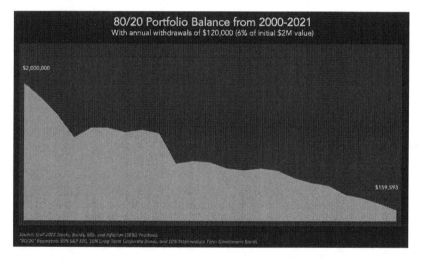

Figure 5.8: Account value after income (2000–2021)

But what if this investor had the exact same return in a different order? In the following example, the returns are exactly the same but arranged in reverse, with the large negative events occurring at the end.

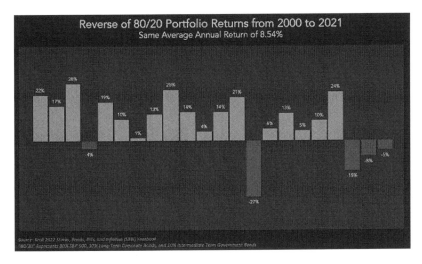

Figure. 5.9: Hypothetical 80/20 portfolio annual returns (2000–2021) in reverse order

If that same retiree started with the same initial balance, the same withdrawal rate and the same average return, how might the different order of returns have impacted the results? As you can see below, the difference is staggering, with the retiree ending up with three times their initial balance, even after taking all that income.

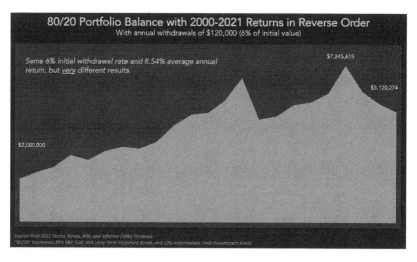

Figure 5.10: Account value after income (2000–2021) returns in reverse order

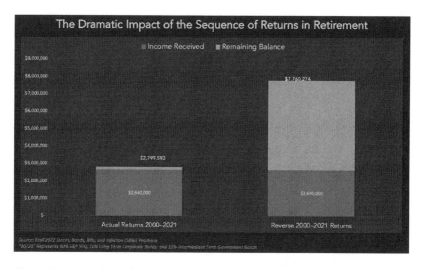

Figure 5.11: Impact of the sequence of returns when taking income

As you can see, timing is everything. Pure luck can be the difference between financial ruin and substantial wealth. This concept is meant to illustrate why it's imperative to diversify sources of income in retirement and not have all your eggs in one basket. It is absolutely not to suggest that any retiree should have all of their investments exposed to this kind of risk in the stock market; rather, it is meant to give a simple representation of how the order of returns (from any source) matters disproportionately in the years right before or right after retirement begins.

So, what can we do to plan for this risk? As discussed already, putting money in cash or overweighting toward bonds at a time like this is unlikely to be the right answer. Staying invested is very important. Study after study has demonstrated that to be the optimal strategy over time. But what if instead of kicking your portfolio when it's down and exacerbating the losses by removing even more from the portfolio, you had an alternate source of income? Something that wasn't correlated with the stock market and would rise regardless of the direction of the market? If we had an asset like that, we could take money from an asset that just went up in value while allowing the investment portfolio to recover like it has every time in the past.

SEQUENCE DEFENSE

Since you cannot know which future you'll be retiring into, you must develop a strategy to weather the worst, but in a way that still works for you during the best. To do so, you can identify or create a *buffer* asset in your portfolio. This will be a place you draw income from in years following a down market.

Before we identify the types of assets that could serve in this capacity, let's look at the concept and how it has impacted safe withdrawal rates over time. The chart in Figure 5.12

below is the same as the safe withdrawal rates chart with level income, but with a twist. In this chart, I told the software to take a year off from taking income from the portfolio in the first __ years following a negative portfolio return.

For example, if in year three the market crashed, then in year four income would come from somewhere else, and we would take zero from the portfolio. If we only had enough to do this once, we would have one year of "volatility buffer" and would then pull income from the portfolio in all subsequent years regardless of market performance. In other scenarios, I tested what safe withdrawal rates would look like if we could take the first two, three or even four negative years off. The results are dramatic, improving some safe withdrawal rates by more than 4%. To put that in perspective, that improvement provides over 40% more income, which makes for an entirely different lifestyle.

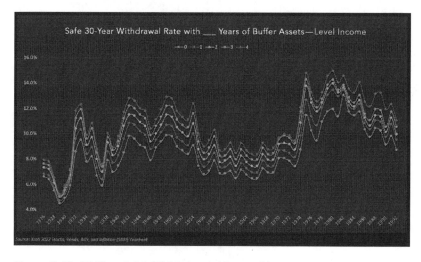

Figure 5.12: 30-Year Initial Withdrawal Rate with Years of Volatility Buffer (Level Income)

By viewing safe withdrawal rates in terms of probability of success, like we did before, adding years of buffer income will dramatically improve the probability that your portfolio will last. Illustrated below, you can see that being able to take even one or two years of income from elsewhere dramatically improves the probability of success. Having the ability to avoid selling low and exacerbating losses clearly has been a strategy that would have historically tamed the sequence of returns risk.

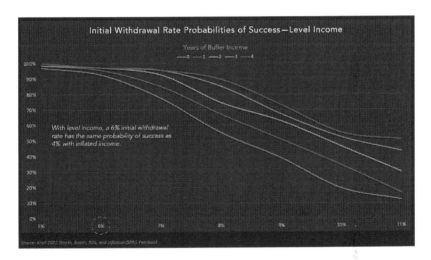

Figure 5.13: Initial Withdrawal Rate Probabilities of Success—
***Level** Income*

The main takeaway of this research is that for every year a retiree was able to pull income from somewhere else, they could have taken about 10% more income from their investment portfolio.

If you can approach your retirement income with a high level of adaptability, you can absolutely take higher initial withdrawal rates and reasonably expect to keep income level throughout retirement. Once again, keeping in mind that if unlikely financial shocks occur, you may need to adjust expectations for the future or pull back on lifestyle expenses for a while. However, if you can also add a volatility buffer to the mix, you'll be in tremendous shape to weather any storm. The following chart (Figure 5.14) shows where retirement income probabilities began with the 4% rule, but how the power of a level-income mindset and the addition of three years of buffer income could improve things. With level income and three years of buffer income, a retiree could roughly *double* their safe withdrawal rate. And that's what your permission-to-spend plan is all about.

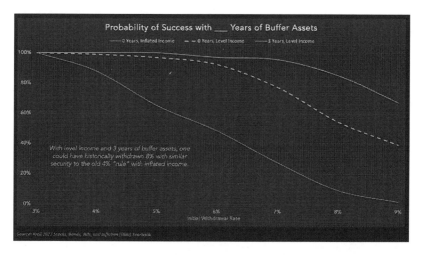

Figure 5.14: The combined impact of level income and buffer assets

SEQUENCE DEFENSE IN ACTION

Taking you back to the sequence-of-returns scenario, let's look again at the real-life scenario of 2000–2021. Imagine a retiree left the workforce in 1999 after the massive stock market gains of the dot-com bubble. With everything in the "new economy" looking promising and different than any time before, she wanted to maintain a heavy allocation toward stocks and high-growth potential investments. Little did she know, she was entering what's been called the "lost decade" of investing, where two massive declines in relatively short succession created an extremely difficult situation for retirees. She began with exactly $2 million and elected to take a level 6% initial annual withdrawal, or $120,000 per year.

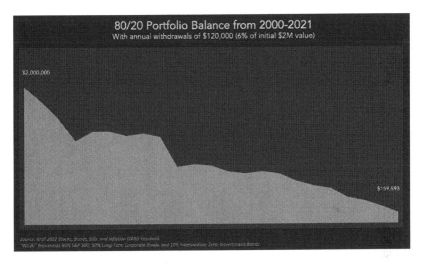

Figure 5.15: Account value after income (2000–2021)

As before, if she were to find herself in this scenario 22 years after retirement, presumably in her 80s when she would be unlikely to go back to work, she would be one market crash away from financial ruin. But since she met with her advisor and had the foresight to build a volatility buffer into the plan, she had alternate sources of income to pull from in the first four years following a down market.

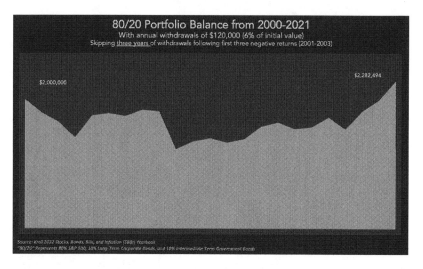

Figure 5.16: Account value after income (2000–2021),
3 years of buffer assets

By having the ability to take income from elsewhere follow-ing the first three down years in the market, her investment account still lost value but was able to recover. She was no longer making the problem worse because she could pull money from other sources that were not correlated with stock market declines. The result was profound, leaving her with almost $2.3 million and a prosperous remainder of retire-ment. Without a plan like this in place, the alternative could have been going broke after starting her retirement as a millionaire.

In the end, none of the scenarios studied provide any guar-antees. Past performance is no guarantee of future results. One must also recognize that this data all comes from roughly the last 100 years in the United States, when it realized unprec-edented economic growth and emerged as the undeniable world superpower. There is no reason that can't continue, but similar studies in other developed economies have shown less rosy outcomes.

Running out of money at an advanced age would be catastrophic. It's the very reason programs like Social Security were developed. The volatility buffer strategy should absolutely be part of the plan, but a prudent retirement income strategy should also include some forms of guaranteed income. In the next chapter, we'll discuss ways to add guarantees to one's income strategy.

Gary was feeling good. He knew he couldn't predict the future, but now understood he needed to remain flexible in his spending and diversify his assets into vehicles that would go up even when the market was going down. We implemented a program to shift a portion of his assets over the next few years to create an alternate source of income. We would meet as a team at least annually to execute the strategy and make sure he was pulling from the right places. As a result, Gary began spending almost twice as much as he was going to on his own, and he hasn't looked back. In fact, he's now several years into retirement with a net worth that's even higher than when he started.

Chapter 6
Three Types of Retirement Paychecks

My friend Zach is a firefighter who married his high school sweetheart, Jenna, a teacher. They both have considerable pensions and are expecting large payouts for life once they have each put enough years into the system. Outside of that, they are building some modest additional savings and investments. One day, I asked Zach and Jenna if they knew they would be forced to take a reduced income in retirement. They seemed perplexed. I told them that while they each have strong pensions, they will not be able to take the full payout because that option would leave their spouse with no income after they die. Nobody had ever brought this up with them before, and it hurt to think about getting less than they were owed. Was there something they could do?

The pandemic of 2020 taught us all a lesson in scarcity. It demonstrated how the availability of seemingly mundane goods or services was not guaranteed. Early on, obtaining masks and sanitizer was nearly impossible after shelves had been cleaned out. Certain items at grocery stores became impossible to obtain due to disruptions in supply chains, which we had all taken for granted only months prior. And then there was the amusing run on toilet paper. When people began to fear that they wouldn't be able to leave the house, many began to hoard toilet paper just in case they weren't able to get it with the regularity they could in the past. The psychology of scarcity, which we're all too familiar with now, can rob a person of their enjoyment in retirement. If you don't know what the future holds, and therefore how long your portfolio will sustain retirement income, you naturally hold back. You hoard the scarce commodity—your money—and avoid spending it in case the aforementioned risks come to pass.

Investment companies who hold your money have no incentive to help you spend. They earn their money by charging fees as a percentage of your investments. If you begin selling investments or taking withdrawals, the amount of money they make from you goes down. I am in no way saying that anyone or any company is trying to cheat or mislead you, but today's retirement system is built on helping you accumulate funds for retirement. Once you get there, it generally remains your job to manage those investments for the long haul and seek ways to derive optimal income.

While the previous discussion of safe withdrawal rates and managing income from investments is applicable to almost all retirees, a sound retirement income plan must include guarantees for at least a portion of the income.

There are generally three ways to obtain guaranteed income in retirement. The first is through the purchase of private annuities from an insurance company. In return for a lump-sum deposit, life insurance companies are prepared to offer you a paycheck for as long as you live.

Second, your employer may offer you a pension in return for years of service. Private companies rarely offer these at the rate they did in the past, but many government employees still enjoy this setup. Pensions will typically offer to pay you (and your spouse) a guaranteed monthly payment for life. Other types of retirement plans are also increasingly adding options that allow you to take your accumulated savings as a stream of guaranteed income.

Third, most employees in the U.S. contribute to the Social Security system. When they get to retirement, they take income based on their lifetime earnings and how long they paid into the system. Unlike most pensions, this income is also indexed for inflation and is a significant piece of most Americans' retirements.

ANNUITIES

Insurance companies pool risk across large numbers of policy holders for risks that would be inefficient or impossible for individuals to insure against on their own. In the case of term life insurance, the company will provide your family with a lump sum in exchange for a relatively modest annual payment. People do this because while the chance of premature death is unlikely, the complete loss of income to one's family would be catastrophic. For a higher annual payment, permanent insurance policies will guarantee a death benefit to be paid to your family when you die, no matter how far into the future that occurs.

With annuities, the math works in reverse. At retirement, for example, the insurance company will accept a lump-sum deposit and in return guarantee income that will last as long as you live. They can do this because their actuaries (mathematicians who apply mortality and investment data to financial products) know on average how long you'll live. They offer contracts to thousands of people just like you, and the law of large numbers says that while they may "lose the bet" and end up paying you for too long, it's likely that someone else died young and they didn't have to pay that person quite as long. Trading a portion of your investments for guaranteed income is a great way to lock in investment gains and get predictable cash flow that you can't outlive.

In its purest form, a single premium immediate annuity (SPIA) will pay a monthly benefit on a single life in return for that single deposit. If that person lives an extremely long time, payments will continue for as long as their life does. On the other hand, if they die shortly after purchasing the annuity, payments stop and the insurance company keeps the remainder of the deposit. The potential for this occurring is unacceptable to a lot of retirees, particularly if they have a spouse or children that would be robbed of that balance. Instead, most individuals choose a variety of other options that ensure benefits continue even if they are not around to collect.

One simple way to guarantee that money is returned is to elect a *cash refund* option. This generally dictates that a beneficiary will receive the difference between the initial deposit and the sum of all benefit payments that have been paid to date. Similarly, some contracts will have a *period certain* option, which guarantees payments will last for no less than a certain number of years, such as 10 or 20. Any of these options will result in a smaller monthly payment to the contract owner in exchange for the certainty that value will continue even in the event of premature death.

Another common approach to annuity income options is to elect a *joint and survivor* option, which provides lifetime income that continues for one's spouse at death. In many cases, purchasers of annuities may choose income for their surviving spouse that is somewhat less than when they're both alive, acknowledging that one mouth requires less income to feed than two. Joint and two-thirds survivor or 50% are two common elections, providing for two-thirds or half of the payout while both were alive, respectively.

An important concept to understand when it comes to annuity survivor options is that you're always going to receive a lower monthly payout in exchange for those after-death guarantees. This is effectively like buying life insurance, paying for these survivor benefits through reduced annuity income. With forethought and advanced planning, particularly for those with good health, you may be able to do better by exploring permanent life insurance options with a qualified retirement income planner.

Deferred income annuities are also an attractive way to guarantee that income starts at a later date. Perhaps upon retirement you have ample funds to cover the first several years before you want guaranteed income to begin. In such a case you could purchase a DIA (deferred-income annuity), with any of the same options listed above, but with payments that begin years into the future.

Taking this concept to the extreme, there are options to have annuities begin paying out at very advanced ages, as a hedge against living too long. One popular form of this is called the QLAC (qualified longevity annuity contract). It allows you to take a limited portion of your IRA assets and purchase a deferred-income annuity that begins as late as age 85. Required minimum distributions don't apply to this portion of your retirement assets. Knowing that a substantial income stream will begin at age 85 can help retirees feel confident about spending more heavily until then.

DEFERRED ANNUITIES

While I've just described how income annuities work, there is a category of annuities that allows you to make systematic or lump-sum deposits to be *annuitized* for income at a later date. These annuities are generally tax-deferred, providing an attractive tax-wrapper, like we discussed in Chapter 3. On top of the tax benefits, popular deferred annuities typically offer additional investment-related guarantees. These guarantees may limit how much you can lose in the market each year while ensuring that, regardless of how well the market performs, your income will be based on growth of a certain percentage when you decide to annuitize for lifetime income.

Have you ever driven over a bridge with very low guardrails and taken your foot off the gas or gripped the steering wheel just a little tighter? Investing in retirement can be scary for many because they can't earn that money back if they suffer losses. But holding back can be quite costly in the long run. Annuities with these guarantees allow conservative investors to add guardrails to their portfolios in a way that allows them to feel more comfortable participating in the stock market. Fees and expenses with these contracts can be high, so it's usually important to implement them with a plan in place for when you'll begin to draw income and reap the benefits.

PENSION INCOME

Even though private corporations are largely moving away from pensions, they are still very much the norm for government and union workers. All pensions are designed differently, but at retirement, they generally share principles that apply to annuities. A common approach is to guarantee an individual a monthly payment that will last the rest of their life. This payment is generally based on a percentage of the employee's final earnings, or an average of their earnings over their last three years of employment.

For example, a pension may prescribe that one will receive 75% of their final income for the remainder of their life, so long as they have given 30 years of service to the company. Those with fewer years of service may still be eligible for pension benefits, but the percentage of final pay would be reduced. In other cases, there may be a formula that gives retirement "credits" based on a combination of years of service and age of the employee. Regardless of how the plan is designed, the employee only needs to put in their time to receive benefits. All management and funding of investments to guarantee those payments remain the sole responsibility of the employer.

A very important thing that anyone eligible for pension benefits should be aware of long before retirement is the available payout options. Unfortunately, I have found that most pensioners never even consider this until the moment they request their retirement paperwork. For married individuals, taking a full pension benefit is typically not a viable option; full pension benefits end upon one's death, leaving a surviving spouse with no income to rely on. To address this, all pensions have survivor options.

For example, if option A is the full benefit with nothing for a survivor, option B may prescribe a lower payout with 50% of benefits payable to a surviving spouse after the death of the primary beneficiary. For an even lower initial payout, one may instead be able to choose option C, which guarantees as much as 100% of benefits payable to the surviving spouse.

Thus, for pensioners who care for their spouse, the choice of taking option A is rarely an option. In fact, federal law generally dictates that a spouse must acknowledge and sign off on any benefits that would leave them nothing upon the death of the primary beneficiary. This is a choice few would make unless there are significant other assets or sources of income available. However, just like with annuities, there are cases where proactive planning ahead of retirement can provide for surviving spouses more efficiently and grant the pensioner permission to take more lucrative monthly payment options.

Pension maximization refers to an old strategy whereby people with pensions purchase permanent life insurance during their working years as a way to alleviate the need to opt for pension reductions. Again, when considering that lower payout in exchange for survivor benefits, the pensioner is effectively buying a form of life insurance by receiving lower income. But what if, ahead of retirement, they could buy a private policy with death benefits that could generate similar value for their spouse if they died prematurely? In such a case, they could take higher payouts from their pension and worry less about what is left for the spouse. They would be in control, and in the much more likely event that they lived a long life, they would receive both the higher income stream and a valuable asset in their retirement plan. This strategy translates to annuity income as well, guaranteeing a financial legacy is left after investment assets are converted to guaranteed lifetime income.

SOCIAL SECURITY

While savings and investments now account for the majority of retirees' income sources, Social Security benefits are still quite important for almost all Americans. The Social Security system generally allows for benefits to begin between the ages of 62 and 70, with reductions or increases in benefits paid depending on whether they begin before or after full retirement age, which is about 67 for retirees going forward. Full retirement age used to be 65, but by the year 2027, after a phaseout period ends, all retirees will have a full retirement age of 67. These benefits can be quite significant, at just over $50,000 in 2022 for the highest earners making over $147,000. Very few will actually get that payout because they would have had to make a high salary for at least 35 years, (historically adjusted for inflation). But even getting most of the way there would result in very significant numbers.

Furthermore, this income is inflation-protected, with annual increases based on changes in the Consumer Price Index (CPI). I mentioned earlier that those of greater means may not need inflation protection for their investment withdrawals, and this is a big reason why. Since Social Security benefits naturally grow, one may be able to take level distributions from investments and still see overall income rise over time. This rising Social Security income mitigates the erosion of inflation on the purchasing power of level investment income, particularly if one defers Social Security payments to achieve the maximum payouts provided by the system.

The timing of starting those benefits is crucial. Entire books and software packages have been written about the optimal strategies for claiming Social Security. Taking benefits later can increase payments by up to 24%. Normal retirement age for most people is now 67, and your benefit payment will increase by 8% for every year you delay claiming until the maximum age of 70. Conversely, taking an early retirement benefit at the earliest age (62) can result in benefits that are nearly half of what they'd be if you had waited until age 70. So, what to do?

Conventional wisdom for most retirees of modest means—particularly married individuals—is that they should wait as long as possible to file for Social Security unless they are aware of a life-shortening condition. Not only will retirement benefits be the highest if you wait, but those benefits will inflate each year from that base. Moreover, upon death, a surviving spouse is entitled to either their own benefit or that of their deceased spouse, whichever is higher. By waiting to maximize income, one is also maximizing survivor benefits for their spouse. Therefore, retirees whose Social Security income makes up a substantial portion of their income should do everything they can to delay payments—perhaps even if that means working an extra year or two.

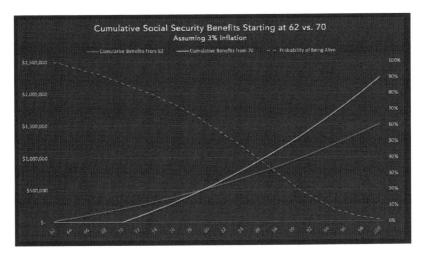

Figure 6.1: Cumulative Social Security Benefits Starting at 62 vs. 70 (Assumes 3% Inflation)

Alternatively, retirees who have accumulated substantial invested wealth and will not heavily rely on Social Security to make ends meet may see things differently. They have paid into a system for their entire working life and can only receive benefits while alive (there is no lump-sum or death-benefit option for Social Security). Since one cannot know how long they'll live, many in this situation may decide to take what's owed to them as early as possible. Taking that a step further, some may view those early payments as a way to keep more of their investments working for them. In Figure 6.2, you can see that if one believes they can earn a modest 6% on their investments, it would be roughly 26 years before waiting until age 70 would have eventually paid off. And in such a case, would a relatively minor eventual disadvantage in one's 90s even be noticed?

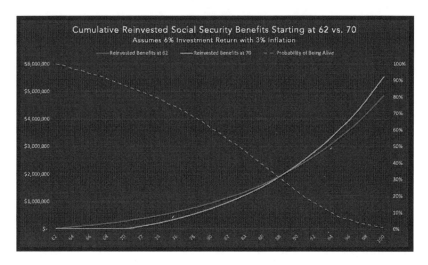

Figure 6.2: Cumulative Reinvested Social Security Benefits Starting at 62 vs. 70

Finding a strategy for claiming Social Security that fits your situation can easily be accomplished with a qualified retirement income strategist who understands the system. Generally speaking, deferring benefits will provide the highest payouts and survivor benefits and alleviate the greatest deal of stress from the later years of your portfolio. But for those who want to get what's owed to them and leave other investments in the market to keep working, an earlier approach may make sense. And since benefits end upon the death of a Social Security beneficiary, even if the retiree doesn't want the income they could use it to purchase permanent life insurance, guaranteeing a lump sum of future benefits for their children.

GUARANTEED INCOME STRATEGY

What's the right amount of guaranteed income in retirement? It's the amount that meets your required expenses and makes you feel comfortable staying invested with the rest, regardless of the market environment. A common approach is called *income flooring*. One subtracts expected Social Security and pension income from their necessary expenses and purchases annuity income to fill in the gap. Necessary expenses obviously include food, housing, transportation and health care, but one could deem a certain level of lifestyle expense as necessary.

With this baseline in place, they are then free to invest the rest for growth and income that enhances their retirement. In fact, with large amounts of guaranteed income coming in the door, they may be more comfortable taking on additional stock market exposure, which I demonstrated in Chapter 2 has historically been extremely rewarding. Thus, their guaranteed retirement income provides them permission to spend, while also granting them permission to remain more fully invested instead of holding back *just in case*.

This discussion of guaranteed income is not just my opinion. It has been studied by the smartest academics in the retirement income planning space, several of whom have been mentors, colleagues and professors of mine. Study after study has demonstrated that people with guaranteed income spend more, are happier in retirement and may even live longer than those without it. In short, not knowing how long you're going to live forces you into a trade-off between spending at a high level and risking running out of money—or spending less and risking under-enjoying your retirement. Guaranteed income that automatically replenishes each month removes the need to make that difficult choice and grants you permission to spend.

So, why doesn't everyone just annuitize their savings? In general, they're worried about two things they lose after they purchase an annuity: *legacy* and *liquidity*. Put differently, if they live a while there will be nothing left over from that lump sum for children, and they lose access to that money if they need it for unforeseen circumstances or the likelihood of requiring long-term care. In the next chapters, I'll describe the best-kept secret in the financial industry. It alleviates all of those concerns, reduces portfolio volatility, minimizes taxation over time and grants retirees permission to spend and enjoy that which has taken them a lifetime to accumulate.

After reviewing Zach and Jenna's payout options, we determined that they could both choose the full benefit if they reworked their life insurance planning today. They already had benefits in place to take care of each other and their two children, but those benefits were temporary. By making those temporary benefits permanent, they could have death benefits in their retirement plan that granted them permission to take the highest payouts without survivor benefits. How to pay for those permanent benefits was their biggest concern, but by creatively shifting other assets around, we were able to add coverage and guarantees while maintaining their available savings and investments.

Chapter 7
Creating Protected Income

Mike and Julia were another typical couple approaching retirement and feeling unprepared. They had dutifully spent the last 20 years raising children, making sacrifices and providing them with every opportunity. In the process, they had neglected to save much for their retirement, and as empty nesters it was catch-up time. Both were maxing out their 401(k) plans at work to accumulate as much as they could. They were focused on retiring in about 10 years, if market returns cooperated with that time frame. They came in wondering if this was the right approach or if there were other places they should be saving their money. They probably couldn't do much more, but was the 401(k) the right place? Were there things about retirement they weren't considering?

You will be afraid to spend. You will also be afraid to annuitize your assets and create a personal pension. You will be afraid because spending too much jeopardizes your ability to leave a financial legacy, pay for long-term care and handle unexpected cash needs in the future. As we've discussed earlier in the book, if you're responsible and care about others these risks will cause you to hold back in case unlikely yet catastrophic events occur.

But what if there was a way to transfer those risks to someone else? What if you could approach retirement and know that no matter what, you will leave at least a certain amount to your family upon your death? What if you knew that potential expensive ongoing care was funded? And what if you had a source of cash outside of your retirement portfolio that you could tap into during volatile markets?

What I'm describing is obviously insurance—but not just any insurance. With most forms of insurance, if you go a long time without bad things happening, you "lose the bet." The insurance company keeps all of the premium. Consider how much you pay for car insurance over the course of your life. You need to have it because if an accident is bad enough, the financial consequences could wipe you out. But for most people, tens of thousands of dollars in premiums are paid over time, from which they never will see any return.

Since insurance policies guard against unlikely events, the policy owner (happily) sees no return in most scenarios. This reality is what causes many people to say they "don't believe" in insurance, or to not purchase enough coverage and essentially gamble that they won't be one of the unlucky few. For many minor forms of insurance, like warranties or protection plans for small electronics, they'd be exactly right. Always decline these extras; the amount you save in total over time will likely far exceed the cost of repair or replacement. However, when it comes to the risks in retirement that I described above, the dollar amounts are much bigger and the consequences could be financially catastrophic. A prudent retiree can't simply choose to gamble with stakes that high. But what if there was a form of insurance that protected against these unlikely yet catastrophic risks, but also built cash value over time and guaranteed to return more than was invested in the plans? I'm about to let you in on the **best-kept secret** in financial planning.

Participating in whole life insurance from a major mutual insurance company is quite possibly the most underappreciated and misunderstood asset in the financial planning realm. Its guarantees, risk/return profile and tax advantages combine to make it a vehicle unlike anything else in the industry. The tax advantages are so good, insurance companies are extremely careful about how it is marketed, fearing that its special treatment will be called into question by Congress. Banks, corporations and wealthy individuals all use it as a tool to manage risk, get predictable returns and minimize taxation over time. In Chapter 8, I'll share how it works as an alternative to traditional "safe" places for one's money, like cash or bonds. However, its insurance properties are what make it such a useful planning tool and something worth Congressional support in the form of tax advantages. What's most important to understand, however, is what its presence in a portfolio does to *other* assets.

The name *whole life* refers to the period of time covered by the death benefit—in other words, your entire life. Thus, unlike cheap term or group life insurance, which is expected to pay out less than 2% of the time, there is an *inevitable gain* of whole life insurance because it pays out *when* you die, not *if* you die. The word *participating* refers to the fact that a policy owner participates in the profitability of the insurance company through policy dividends paid annually.

Ever wonder why so many insurance companies have the word *mutual* in their name? It's because those companies typically have a different ownership structure, where the company operates for the benefit of its policy owners instead of share-holders. There are no shareholders demanding quarterly profits or other return on investment. Rather, mutual companies pass their profitability through to their policy owners in the form of policy dividends, making their interests aligned over long periods of time.

When determining what premiums to collect for whole life policies, companies make assumptions about *mortality* (when they expect people to die, on average), *expenses* (the administrative costs of servicing a policy over time) and *interest rates* (what the company can earn on its conservatively invested reserves). Since these premiums are guaranteed and can never be changed, the company will set prices based on what they assume to be the worst-case scenario. Thus, they are intentionally overcharging policy owners to ensure they can honor their guarantees.

This is a good thing. You're buying insurance that you'll own for several decades or more, so you want to be sure the company can follow through on its promises. But recall the value of a mutual company. When the worst-case scenario doesn't happen and they outperform their dire assumptions, the company generates a profit that gets passed back to the policy holders they operate for the benefit of. This arrangement is entirely unique to whole life insurance—and is also what is most misunderstood about it. Premiums for whole life insurance tend to be higher than alternative forms of permanent insurance, but you get what you pay for. Historically, the participation in company dividends and profitability has made whole life insurance the most valuable form of coverage by a long shot.

A unique feature of whole life policies is their guaranteed cash values. Policy cash values are guaranteed to rise in value each year until they eventually equal the death benefit at age 100 or 121. This is true whether the insurance company pays a dividend or not, and these values are typically guaranteed to grow to more than the total premiums paid. But the major mutual companies have always paid dividends, with some paying dividends in consecutive years dating all the way back to the Civil War. So, it's not really a question of *if* you'll get a dividend, but *how much* to expect based on interest rates.

Policy dividends can be taken in cash or to reduce ongoing premiums. Most commonly, they are reinvested back into policies to make their values grow and compound over time. The biggest driver of long-term dividend performance is the interest component, representing what the company is earning on its conservative investments and profitability from subsidiaries. The dividend interest rate will therefore rise and fall with the prevailing interest rate environment, but it will generally offer much more competitive rates than other guaranteed assets due to the nature of those investments. (Much more on that in Chapter 8.) This annual interest in the form of a policy dividend provides tremendous upside potential, as well as a likely hedge against inflation because interest rates have historically tended to correlate with inflation. As rates rise, so will cash values and death benefits.

Long-term care insurance has been around for decades, but the market has shifted dramatically in recent years. As described in Chapter 4, long-term care is ongoing care that isn't covered by any traditional medical plan or Medicare. The costs can easily carry six-figure annual price tags. While most of the time this care is short-lived, for some unfortunate folks it can last several years or longer and threaten the finances of not only their own retirement plan, but also the welfare of their extended family, who may feel obligated to provide care or help cover costs. Thus, long-term care coverage is not just about softening the financial blow of a potential need but about allowing for one to age with dignity on their own terms.

Long-term care insurance used to be rather inexpensive, costing maybe a couple thousand dollars per year in exchange for six-figure annual benefits that could potentially last a lifetime. As the industry has matured, life expectancies have lengthened and companies have realized how many people keep and claim on these policies, costs have risen dramatically. Many companies that used to sell these contracts have simply left the business due to the uncertainty and huge risk involved.

When insurance companies, the masters of making calculated bets, don't even want to offer a product because they think it might end up in losses, that's all you need to know about it potentially being a good deal for you. The problem is that modern long-term care insurance policies have gotten so expensive that it is unreasonable for most retirees to rely on them to cover the entirety of potential costs. It could cost tens of thousands of dollars annually to do so, at which point most would rather roll the dice and attempt to self-insure.

However, a shift has occurred over the last decade or so, whereby major life insurers have created hybrid policies that allow owners of permanent life insurance to add riders to their policies that grant access to the death benefits *while alive*—essentially receiving benefits early that were expected to be paid down the road anyway. This allows insurers to control how much risk they are taking and provide access to values for policy owners very inexpensively.

Some newer, very popular policy designs actually suppress death-benefit and cash-value growth in exchange for higher long-term care benefits, guaranteeing one's money back at surrender or death. Regardless of what your advisor recommends, the idea with modern long-term care insurance is to create a reasonably large enough pool of funds to soften the financial blow and provide options so you're not forced into difficult decisions that place undue stress on your family and finances. With a life insurance hybrid design, you can be sure that even if you're one of the many who likely won't need expensive ongoing care, you'll have cash values and death benefits that guarantee a return on the premiums you've paid. Instead of the use-it-or-lose-it nature of almost all forms of insurance, this is really use-it-or-use-it. It's just a matter of how and when.

YOUR PERMISSION SLIP: THE PROTECTED INCOME PROCESS

Threats, opportunities and obligations. These are the reasons people cling to their cash and are afraid to spend. They worry about the potential "what ifs" in their retirement and the threat of the need for cash to pay for unforeseen expenses. They may also have FOMO (fear of missing out) and are afraid to annuitize or spend money that could have remained invested for the opportunity of achieving some higher rate of return. But most importantly, retirees generally feel obligated to others—whether that's their spouse, children or community interests. At the very least, they owe it to their spouse to ensure some money is left over after their passing. But they commonly also have goals of leaving at least modest sums to their children, church or charitable interests. Therefore, to take control and feel free to spend, they must address their reasons for holding back.

Imagine two married retired couples, both age 65. One couple has exactly $1 million invested for retirement. Otherwise, they own their home and have modest savings—those investments are all they have on top of Social Security. The second couple in our example has only $800,000 invested alongside a similar home and savings. But the husband also has a $600,000 permanent life insurance policy with a long-term care benefit that allows them to use the death benefit early if they require care. Both retired couples have the goal of maximizing their income while alive, providing for their spouse and ensuring money is available to pay for care, with hopes there is something left over for their children. How differently do you think they each would approach their retirement?

	Retirement A	Retirement B
Savings & Investments	$1,000,000	$800,000
Whole Life Insurance Death Benefit with LTC Rider	$0	$600,000
Whole Life Cash Value	$0	$100,000
Total Cash + Investments	$1,000,000	$900,000

Figure 7.1: Retired Couple A vs. Retired Couple B

If you look at the bottom line above, you may feel like the first retiree is in better shape due to having $100,000 more cash plus investments on hand. But remember our discussion of safe withdrawal rates in Chapter 5. Retirees in the first situation will be afraid to spend—as they should be. Expensive long-term care or a poor sequence of market returns could spell disaster and cause the money to run out before retirement is over.

An annuity would guarantee income lasts forever, but then there would be no legacy for children and no reserve for potential long-term care expenses. Their only choice (unless they compromise on their stated goals) is to hold back and keep some money in reserve. On top of all that, these retirees will be afraid to see their investments dip below $1 million because of the need for it to last until the last one dies. The 4% rule and spending based on worst-case potential outcomes will definitely apply for these retirees.

The couple in the second situation will feel much better about spending. They could even turn their retirement account into a pension by using an annuity. At the time of this writing, a single life annuity would provide 6.5% cash flow to a 65-year-old male; meaning he could turn $800,000 into a stream of $52,000 of income he couldn't outlive. Every month, a fresh $4,333 would be deposited into his checking account alongside his Social Security payments, without any concern for those payments stopping. He would have permission to spend as much as he wanted, knowing more was on the way just 30 days later.

If the husband died prematurely, income from the annuity would stop, but a tax-free death benefit of $600,000 would be paid to the surviving spouse. This $600,000 is about the same as the after-tax value of the $800,000 in investments, assuming tax rates are about 25%. Since the surviving spouse could purchase her own annuity with the proceeds, she's covered for life as well. Interestingly, her death benefit needs actually go down each year due to the fact that annuity payout rates improve the older she gets. Figure 7.2 shows the tax-free death benefit she would need to purchase an annuity that produces the same after-tax income of the annuity today. In the most likely event that they both live a while, excess death benefits will grow to become part of their financial legacy, or they could provide inflation-adjusted survivor income.

Additionally, whole life death benefits generally rise over time, creating even more security and generational wealth transfer.

Age	Survivor Annuity Payout Rate	Death Benefit Needed
66	6.3%	$619,638
70	7.0%	$557,748
75	8.4%	$465,549
80	10.3%	$377,161
85	13.6%	$286,192
90	17.8%	$219,476

Figure 7.2: Payout Rate and Death Benefit Needed

So, let's go back to our two retired couples. But instead of looking at their assets, let's look at their *income*, which is all that really matters when it comes to one's lifestyle in retirement. Because the retired husband in Retirement B knows his wife has survivor income, there is cash on hand for emergencies, and he can access death benefits for long-term care, he feels free to annuitize the entire retirement account and get a 6.5% payout, or $52,000 for life, guaranteed.

The couple with Retirement A must live according to worst-case assumptions while also holding money in reserve *just in case*. Furthermore, if they need to use that money, they're invading principal and putting the remainder of their retirement in great jeopardy. I'm being fair below, but if they put aside a quarter of their assets in a rainy-day fund, that means a quarter of their income would need to go away as well.

	Retirement A	Retirement B
Savings & Investments	$1,000,000	$800,000
Whole Life Insurance Death Benefit with LTC Rider	$0	$600,000
Whole Life Cash Value	$0	$100,000
Total Cash + Investments	$1,000,000	$900,000
Initial Income	$40,000	$52,000
Guaranteed for Life	No	Yes
Available Sources of Cash*	No	Yes
Initial Value at Death	$750,000	$600,000

Figure 7.3: Retired Couple A vs. Retired Couple B, Continued with income

*NOTE: Invading principal would require a retiree to reduce income to maintain the same probability of success.

The concept above was kept extremely simple on purpose. Of course, real life can often be much more complex, which is why you should always work with a qualified financial advisor to talk through the nuances of your individual plan. That said, the takeaway should be quite clear. To the extent you can own participating whole life insurance in your portfolio, the greater comfort you will have spending the remainder of your assets. You don't necessarily need to have everything covered, but the presence of guaranteed death benefits, a pool of funds to pay for long-term care and an unrestricted pile of cash allows you to more freely spend the rest of your assets. Few retirees would choose to turn their entire life savings into a pension, but many choose to do so with a significant portion, covering basic living expenses with this income and funding lifestyle goals with investments and other sources of income.

I call this my *Protected Income Process* because it redirects finances to produce the most income during retirement while meeting obligations, preparing for threats and still allowing the opportunity for growth. We don't want to go into retirement acting as our own insurance company; we want to shift that risk elsewhere so we can free up our money for what it was intended to do. But that's only part of the equation. With those risks off the table, Chapter 8 will discuss the magical way you can use participating whole life cash values to accumulate wealth and increase your spending power.

> *Mike and Julia acknowledged that they'd have a tough time feeling comfortable spending in retirement. They knew they wanted to take care of each other, plan for long-term care and provide a small legacy. There would likely be enough money for this, but without any plan in place or guarantees, they would be afraid to spend. Instead of blindly saving more and more into the same accounts, they decided to add a strategic asset to their portfolio. This asset wouldn't necessarily yield a larger balance at retirement, but the guarantees and insurance benefits put them in control and at ease with spending their other assets. They even moved a portion of their money to a deferred annuity to take advantage of income riders that would eventually create a guaranteed floor of income.*

Chapter 8
The Best-Kept Secret

Chris was one of the most conservative clients I have ever come across. He was an electrical engineer and very intelligent, but he came from extremely humble beginnings and was extraordinarily risk averse. Losing meaningful amounts of money was not something he could witness and still sleep at night. He had some investments through his retirement plan at work, as well as a mountain of cash. I recall congratulating him on his saving habits, but it was painful for me to see so much investment potential go to waste. These savings were earning next to no interest in the bank, and the little bit of interest he was earning was taxable. Inflation would continue to eat away at the purchasing power of those dollars, making them lose their value in real terms. How could I help him put that cash to work while still maintaining access and guarantees?

What is your strategy for safe, accessible money? Few ever really consider their cash position as strategic or as something worthy of a great deal of attention. Many also view a large cash position as wasteful, wrongfully believing that money should be invested in other opportunities. This is what is referred to as *opportunity cost*, where the cost of holding cash is the foregone potential gains of investing elsewhere. But what if you could get attractive, risk-free returns on your cash without taxation? I'm about to let you in on the best-kept secret in financial planning.

Most attention in the financial services industry goes toward investments, with lofty retirement projections and fancy charts and graphs about historical performance. It's all very exciting and fun to talk about. Typical client reports will show how adjustments to saving rates and investment allocations will compound over time, with ranges of potential values and probabilities of success. However, for the average investor working with an advisor, investments are very much a commodity. This means that you're generally going to be well diversified across the same major asset classes regardless of which advisor you choose to work with, assuming equal qualifications and experience. It's impossible to predict the future, and most advisors will offer similar advice just like most doctors will offer a similar diagnosis and treatment plan.

Cash allocations are often ignored by financial advisors, leaving clients to use traditional banks for this portion of their portfolio. With interest rates on savings so low, holding cash today can mean missing out on a lot of compound interest over time. Federal Direct Insurance Corporation (FDIC) protection may be attractive, but short of a Great Depression–style run on the bank, you're paying one heck of a lot in terms of lost opportunities for that money to get that protection. This may be particularly true in times of high inflation. At the time of this writing, inflation was at its highest in over 40 years. This drives down the purchasing power of a dollar. Five percent annual inflation means that next year $1,000 will purchase only $950 worth of the same goods it could purchase today. The next year it's $903. The next it's $857. You get the idea.

With all that said, every prudent financial plan needs a readily available cash allocation. During one's working years, this allocation can be viewed simply as an emergency fund or as money that can be used for investment opportunities. It needn't be huge, because working individuals may also have available credit that can be tapped and repaid in later years with earned income. In retirement, however, much greater amounts of stable cash need to be there so one isn't forced to sell investments low during a bear market. I discussed this in greater detail in Chapter 5. I talked about sequence-of-returns risk and needing an alternate source of funds from which to pull income. Using credit makes no sense in this situation, because without future earned income to pay that debt down, repayment will have to come from the sale of investments. This forces the retiree into trying to time the market, which is very risky and generally a fool's errand.

A riskier alternative to cash is bond funds. Over the last several decades, the bond market has been a phenomenal place to hold one's more conservative investments due to the declining interest rate environment. This is no longer true. As detailed in Chapter 4, we are sitting in an all-time low interest rate environment. From here we can expect paltry returns on bonds at best, and volatility or losses at worst. That isn't to say one shouldn't hold some in their portfolio for diversification, but they absolutely should not be viewed as a liquid, stable source of funds to be used to meet living expenses. During stock market declines, bond markets can simultaneously lose value. One needs an asset in their portfolio that is not correlated with traditional asset classes they can count on to rise no matter what.

So, what is a prudent retiree to do? If cash in the bank is no good, and other conservative investments carry too much risk, then how does one effectively allocate their funds? How does one create the volatility buffer (described in Chapter 5) to allow them to spend their other assets more freely and potentially take even greater risks? Well, I'm going to let you in on a secret that few understand and one that insurance companies are very careful not to draw too much attention to.

THE BEST "BORING" MONEY CAN BUY

For the many reasons this book has already outlined, we all need boring, accessible, stable assets in our portfolios, particularly in retirement. Participating whole life insurance can provide this better than anything else commonly available. Here's how it works.

1. Premiums are paid to the participating whole life insurance company.

2. The company issues a whole life insurance contract.

   a) The contract guarantees that cash values will rise every year.

   b) Cash values will not be taxed as they grow.

3. Premiums are held in reserve and invested by the insurance company.

4. When income from their investments exceeds guarantees, the participating whole life insurance company pays a dividend.

    a)   Better than assumed mortality or expenses also contribute to dividends.

5. Dividends are reinvested into the contract, compounding growth.

6. If it meets IRS guidelines, cash values are available at any time, income tax-free.

The magic of participating whole life insurance is that, through the contract, you get to indirectly participate in the performance of the insurance company's general investment account, where the company has guaranteed away all market risk. Cash values generally must increase each year, no matter what. At the same time, Congress has blessed whole life insurance with favorable tax treatment that makes it possible to receive future gains income tax-free.

These are tax advantages with few limitations, meaning you can generally contribute as much as the insurance company and IRS guidelines will allow. You can access that money whenever you want without age restrictions, such as having to wait until age 59½ to avoid penalties or being forced to take required minimum distributions at age 72. And since you get to participate in the performance of the company's investment portfolio without any potential for loss, you may get better risk-adjusted returns than you could possibly dream of in a similarly constructed portfolio of your own. Insurance charges and policy fees are certainly present, but the lack of volatility and favorable tax treatment outweigh those costs in my experience.

These aren't cocktail-party returns, where you're bragging to friends over drinks about the 50% gain you just realized. But these are brag-worthy returns when comparing them to what you can earn after tax in other assets that are guaranteed or at least considered very conservative. All of these elements combine to make participating whole life insurance the ideal asset to act as a volatility buffer and alternate source of income in times of market turmoil.

So, what's the catch? If this is such an amazing asset for your safe money, why doesn't everyone own it?

It really isn't complicated. There are two "catches" when it comes to participating whole life insurance. The first catch is that you must be healthy enough to get it. Life insurance is medically underwritten, meaning you must satisfactorily answer a series of questions about your medical history and submit clean blood and urine samples. Unless you have serious medical conditions or severe weight issues, this is generally not a problem and will not preclude you from getting a great deal. Policies are issued with various health ratings that do impact performance, but as long as you're at least in average health, your performance should be fine. That being said, the younger you are when you add it to your portfolio, the less likely you are to have developed the kind of conditions that would cause an insurance underwriter to decline or offer substandard coverage.

The other catch is patience, because the costs of an insurance policy are generally front-loaded. By structuring contracts this way, the insurance company knows they can meet guarantees, cover costs and provide maximum long-term value. Within just a few years for a typical policy, your cash value will be rising by more than your contribution. Break-even points occur a handful of years later, at which point the "funding phase" of the contract is complete, and your policy is in a mature state without being encumbered by most administrative costs.

In general, after about 8–10 years, your policy should be growing at about 80–90% of the full stated dividend interest rate, all totally income tax-free and without risk of going down. The only question is how much it goes up each year based on that stated dividend interest rate. In 2022, the biggest, oldest mutual companies are generally paying dividends between 5% and 6%. These rates are the lowest they've been in about 50 years and have been in the double-digits during the high interest rate environment of the 1980s. Most savers would do anything to get 80–90% of these current dividend rates—particularly if they're not paying taxes and there's no risk of loss.

You might be wondering how insurance companies are able to offer such high dividend interest rates, particularly in an environment like this. Each year, billions of dollars of premium payments come in the door to pay for permanent life insurance contracts, for which the company promises to pay death benefits decades down the road. Insurance regulations require that they must hold a great deal of this money in reserve to meet those future obligations. If you look at the financial ratings of the major mutual life insurance companies, they are almost always top-shelf because they make such strong guarantees and hold so much in reserves. The top asset classes within their portfolios are generally bonds and mortgages, stable assets and a mix of other diversifying assets. These asset classes are sometimes referred to as *fixed income*, meaning the investor can expect a guaranteed rate of income from that investment.

For example, a bond is essentially a loan to a corporation or government. An insurance company may offer to loan a company $100 million in exchange for 5% interest, payable each year. Therefore, their fixed income is $5 million per year.

At the bond's maturity—perhaps 20 years from now—the entire $100 million is returned to the insurance company with the final interest payment.

Historically, insurance companies have held most of their investments in long-term bonds, mortgages and other fixed-income securities. In higher interest rate environments, the fixed income they expect from those investments is much higher—as was the case over the last several decades. Because a company has new predictable cash flow each year from annual premium payments, it continually makes similar new investments at current interest rates. Thus, its portfolio income represents an average of what long-term corporate bonds have paid over the last decade or so.

Generally speaking, individuals would have a hard time investing this way. The trade-off with bonds (or CDs at the bank) is liquidity versus yield. To obtain the highest rates from bonds (or CDs), one must tie up their money for very long periods of time. But because an insurance company is investing to back guarantees that won't be paid out for many decades to come, they aren't interested with liquidity. They're able to meet their cash needs using incoming cash flow, income from other investments, maturing securities, or cash reserves.

Individuals need to be able to sell their investments to fund their lifestyle, because living off of the interest isn't really a viable strategy in a low interest rate environment like today's. Furthermore, in Chapter 4 we discussed the threat to bonds if interest rates rise. If rates rise sharply and an investor needs to sell, they may get far less than what they paid for that bond. An insurance company is not concerned with today's market value of their bonds—they will simply continue to hold them, collect interest until maturity and reinvest them once they mature. No need to sell at a loss. So, the insurance company is insulated from interest rate risk and simply passes through its *portfolio average* to the policy owner via the dividend.

Many companies also have significant investments in common and preferred stocks. These stocks are not generally the household names you hear about on TV; rather, they represent strategic investments and subsidiaries of the insurance company. Over the last several decades, most of the largest mutual life insurance companies have invested a portion of their reserves into other profitable businesses. As those businesses turn profits, they pay a portion of that profitability to their shareholders (the mutual life insurance company) in the form of dividends. And because the mutual life insurance company operates for the benefit of the policy owner, they pass through a portion of that investment return to policy owners via life insurance policy dividends. Thus, the modern dividend interest rate is a combination of the fixed-income portfolio average rate with an enhancement from these other business earnings.

In higher interest rate environments, this can be helpful. But it has stood out as particularly game-changing in the recent low interest rate environment. As yields on fixed-income investments have consistently come down over the last few decades, the increasing impact of these other business earnings has allowed dividend interest rates to remain buoyant.

Putting all of that together, the dividend interest rate on a participating life insurance contract represents a much higher rate than an individual could obtain on their own without taking on a lot of risk. The insurance company, through the contractually guaranteed cash-value increases, removes all market volatility for the policy owner and allows them to indirectly participate in the income the insurance company is earning on their investments. Therefore, once a policy is somewhat mature, risk-adjusted returns are astonishing. Through long-term ownership of participating whole life insurance, one has been able to obtain bond-like returns but without risk, volatility, taxes or the need to wait to access funds. Unlike the trade-off between liquidity and yield for traditional fixed-income vehicles described above, a mature whole life contract's dividend provides a rolling average of the long end of the yield curve but near-complete liquidity.

ACCESSING CASH VALUE

The real *magic* of participating whole life insurance is one's ability to get their money income tax-free with minimal rules or restrictions. Permanent life insurance cash value has two major tax advantages. First, owners of qualifying policies are allowed to get their cost basis—the sum of all premiums paid—back first before they have to recognize any gain.

This means that if you pay $100,000 into the policy over time, you can withdraw that much or *surrender* a portion of your policy to obtain that much and owe nothing in taxes. This is different than almost all other investment vehicles with tax advantages, as they generally force you to recognize gains *first* before you get your principal back. However, if you withdraw more than your total investment from a life insurance contract or cash in the whole thing, you will owe ordinary income taxes on any gains.

But wait, there's more.

Policy loans are the secret sauce of permanent life insurance plans. They are what allow individuals to receive many times their investment entirely free from taxation. They are not treated as taxable transactions by the IRS because there is an expectation that they will be paid back at interest. The insurance company will typically allow you to borrow up to about 95% of your policy's cash value at any time. When you do this, you will be charged an interest rate on that money, payable to the life insurance company. This may sound like a bad deal. Who wants to borrow against their own money, at interest? However, you're borrowing against a policy cash value that will also continue to *earn* interest, usually at similar rates to what you're paying in interest on the loan.

Recall that whole life policy dividend interest rates represent a rolling average of what one may expect to earn in bonds over time. Policy loan rates for many major companies are based on an index called the Moody's Seasoned Corporate Bond Yield. It is a proxy for the rate at which major insurance companies are making current fixed-income investments. So, loan rates and dividend interest rates should rise and fall together over long periods of time, which has historically been the case.

Interest rates aside, the additional beauty of the policy loan is that it is unstructured. You needn't pay it back on any set schedule, or maybe ever. So long as the loan balance remains below the total cash value of the policy, the insurance company doesn't care about getting repaid. They will simply wait until the permanent death benefit is paid when you die and subtract the balance from the total. Thus, your tax-free death benefit is paying off your loan for you, with the remainder going to your beneficiaries.

So, one could purchase a permanent life insurance policy at a relatively young age, get to retirement and withdraw all of their contributions income tax-free, switch to policy loans and continue to draw against the policy without owing any income taxes—so long as they ensure there is a positive cash value balance at all times. Furthermore, none of this income is reported to the IRS and will therefore not impact the taxation of other assets or income sources, as is the case with some other tax-advantaged vehicles. This is one of the greatest tax advantages still available to the common investor.

Be Your Own Bank

While the focus of this book is on participating whole life insurance as your strategic backstop and permission slip, it is also an incredibly valuable asset during your accumulation phase.

Due to the policy loan mechanics mentioned above, many investors and business owners (including me) use their cash value for opportunities throughout their life instead of traditional banks. Being able to borrow against your cash value at rates equal to or lower than its growth rate means you're making money on that cash value even while you've put it to use elsewhere. This is referred to as *positive arbitrage*, and while not guaranteed, it has historically been available to owners of mature whole life contracts. The idea is to build cash value, borrow against the policy, pay that policy back and repeat the process over and over as time goes by. All along, the contract continues to build value as though those loans never took place, and any outstanding loans are collateralized by that cash value. Since adjustable loan rates rise and fall with dividend interest rates over time, the risk of things going wrong is minimal if you're keeping an eye on it in the short term and servicing the policy debt. It's important to note that life insurance policies are not banks, nor are the companies that issue them. FDIC insurance is not available, which is why buying from the largest, oldest high-performing companies is prudent.

BUYER BEWARE

Of course, with tax advantages for cash value life insurance this good, one would expect there to be a broad market with a variety of alternatives to whole life insurance. These alternatives are all forms of "universal life." They allow for more flexible premiums but shift all of the performance risk to the policy owner. There are three primary types to be aware of, and they have evolved in response to market conditions in the order below.

Current Assumption Universal Life (UL)

Popularized in the 1980s, this type of contract took advantage of the high interest rates of the time. Illustrations of future policy values were made at prevailing savings rates of the time, using double-digit interest rates as "conservative" projections of the future. As rates continued to fall steadily after the peak of the early 1980s, policies that relied on the higher interest rates of the past began to fail; they would lapse before policy owners could do anything to stop them. These are rarely sold anymore.

Variable Universal Life (VUL)

In the wake of falling interest rates during one of the greatest stock markets in history (spanning from the 1980s to the 1990s), VUL became a popular way to get the tax advantages of permanent life insurance while being invested in the market. Inside these policies, owners would direct their cash value to be invested in various funds or market indices to capture the upside of the market. Policy projections showed very high assumptions for returns—because that's all investors of the time could recall. It was the "new economy," with technology paving the way for a new future.

But of course, what goes up must come down. VUL contract owners suffered severe losses in the years following the dot-com bubble. These contracts are still sold and can absolutely work. But getting money out can be tricky and fraught with risk, due to market timing.

Indexed Universal Life (IUL)

Following two major market crashes within one decade (2000–02 and 2008), IUL exploded in popularity with the promise of "upside potential with downside protection." To make this claim, it ties its performance to a stock market index such as the S&P 500 while guaranteeing minimum crediting of 0% regardless of how far the stock market falls. The trade-off is a cap on performance, limiting policy performance to a certain percentage, such as 10%. That upside cap is typically not guaranteed; it has fallen quite a bit over the last several years, and most companies reserve the right to bring it down to as low as 3%. Furthermore, as with all of these universal life policies, insurance charges can be raised at the company's discretion. The end result is a good sales pitch and policy owners carrying all of the risk.

With hundreds of alternative plans available and some great advisors in the mix, these alternatives to whole life insurance may sometimes be a good fit. However, one needs to understand that as the policy owner, they bear all of the risk. If the policy underperforms, the owner must contribute even more capital to the plan to make up for it, or projections will not occur as illustrated. Annual caps on crediting rates may make it difficult or impossible to recover from particularly bad markets. Taking money out will also be an administrative challenge in these plans no matter what.

In the end, whole life insurance's guarantees shift all of the risk to the company, ensuring that it will be there to serve as the backstop, permission slip and strategic asset. The only question is by how much the policy will exceed guarantees. Such attractive risk-adjusted returns allow investors to take bigger calculated risks in their investment portfolios, where the risk should actually live. Don't gamble with what is supposed to be the cornerstone of your family's financial security.

Over the course of several years, Chris transformed his pile of inefficient, taxable cash into an overfunded whole life policy that he now considers his bank. He currently has nothing in his savings account because he's earning over 5% per year in this new policy, income tax-free. In fact, he used its cash value recently for a down payment on his first investment property, and he's actively replenishing it for future goals and investments. In retirement, this will be the safe, accessible asset that gives him the comfort and freedom to remain more fully invested in the market with everything else. Since he and I first met, Chris has gotten married. He enjoys having the death benefit to protect his wife, as well. Putting his cash to work has resulted in tens of thousands of dollars in additional net worth that he wouldn't have had if the money was still sitting in the bank, and it will compound to be hundreds of thousands in retirement.

Chapter 9
Designing Your Permission Slip

Nicole was one of the most well-educated clients I had come across. She and her husband, Kevin, were approaching retirement and had done a fair amount of research on retirement strategies. It was clear to them that they favored a safety-first approach like the one described in this book, but they didn't know where to start or who to talk to. They were referred by a mutual CPA friend who knew my firm specialized in this type of work. Nicole and Kevin knew they were conservative and wanted to make sure their children and loved ones were taken care of, but their situation was complex, and defining a strategy was a challenge.

By now, you should clearly see the advantages of participating whole life insurance and how its inclusion in your portfolio can put you in control. First, permanent death benefits guarantee that there will be money left over for your loved ones, regardless of how much you spend or how financial markets might impact the value of your savings. Adding a long-term care insurance component is also prudent. It protects against the immense financial risk that a prolonged need for ongoing, expensive care can present. Wealthy individuals worth several million dollars or more may be able to absorb many of these costs, but the average investor is generally ill prepared to do so.

It's all about options and flexibility. This coverage puts you in control of desired outcomes and ensures you won't be a burden to your family. And finally, the cash value of whole life insurance can be a "better bond" in retirement, offering bond-like returns but none of the volatility, taxation or restrictions that come with traditional retirement accounts. Its presence in your portfolio may increase your comfort with taking more risk elsewhere and giving yourself the best chance at meaningful investment returns.

When considering how much permanent death benefit you want, it helps to first consider how much you want to guarantee will be left to beneficiaries upon your death. Many clients tend to say that leaving a large legacy to children isn't actually a primary goal and that their kids can just have whatever is left over. But when pressed, they admit they'd feel sad if nothing were left behind.

What's the minimum amount you'd like to ensure passes to your beneficiaries or other charitable interests? With that number in mind, now consider how much after-tax *income* you want to ensure your spouse is left with if you were to die before them. An easy place to start is simply by looking at how much of your portfolio you intend to annuitize, turning it into a pension. To guarantee an equal income stream for your spouse after your death, you need a death benefit that is at least as much as the after-tax value of the money you intend to annuitize.

For example, if you intend to take $400,000 to buy a lifetime stream of income, and we assume taxes on that income are roughly 25%, then a death benefit of about $300,000 (25% less than $400,000) could purchase enough income to last the rest of your spouse's life. Annuity payout rates are based on gender and age, and the older you are, the more annual income you will receive. That said, you or your spouse may not be concerned with having the same income after the other's death—one mouth is easier to feed than two, after all. The choice is yours. In a retirement with ample savings, this is all about wants and desired outcomes, not needs. By adding this number to the amount you want to leave as a legacy, you have your minimum permanent death benefit requirement.

But we're not done yet. If your last name isn't Rockefeller, chances are it makes sense to plan for potential long-term care costs. A simple rider can be added to your policy, giving you access to the death benefit while you're still alive to mitigate the impact of an expensive claim on your assets. You generally needn't worry about covering the maximum possible claim, but it's theoretically unlimited. Think of it like co-insurance. You're going to be footing many of the bills from cash flow, income and existing savings, but extra money will take the pressure off.

In 2022, access to a pool of $250,000–$500,000 is a wonderful plan that should cover several years of care in most markets. For those who can't medically qualify for permanent life insurance, more and more income annuities are available these days that do not require underwriting and provide extra benefits in the event you require care. These are becoming increasingly popular for people who aren't concerned with leaving any legacy behind. The trade-off, of course, is lower annuity payouts than one might expect without such protections.

Last, you need to build a strategic source of cash during market downturns. All participating whole life insurance contracts naturally build cash value, but some do it more quickly than others. At retirement, you ideally want to have at least two to three years of income you can pull from an alternate source, although any little bit helps. This translates to about 10–15% of your overall portfolio that you'll want in cash value. Instead of focusing on the size of your contribution to a whole life plan, you should focus on the projected percentage of your at-retirement portfolio its cash value will represent. A qualified insurance advisor should be able to help you design a policy that meets all of the goals listed above. In the event you are retiring shortly, it will take a little time to build cash value. Death and long-term care benefits can be purchased immediately, but you'll want to hold a bit more cash in the bank as you start the cash transformation process toward whole life becoming your bank.

FINDING THE MONEY

It's easy to get sticker shock when reviewing the premium requirements of permanent life insurance plans, particularly participating whole life insurance. These contracts guarantee that you'll get more money back from the insurance company no matter what happens, whether it's via cash value while you're alive, long-term care benefits if you require care or the inevitable gain of the death benefit. Therefore, you cannot think of it as a payment. Instead, for this to make sense, you need to think of this as just another financial account that you're transferring money to. Depending on your age and asset mix, the source of those funds can vary.

In the best-case scenario, you're reading this book at least several years before retirement, while still employed. The younger you are when you buy whole life insurance, the bigger the benefits, the lesser the internal charges and the better the opportunity for compound interest to be your friend. In that case, the premium can come largely from income. Examine how you're currently saving. If you're maxing out your 401(k), I suggest you consider contributing only up to the amount your employer matches and redirecting those extra contributions into a whole life insurance plan. You want to keep funding up to the amount your employer matches because that's free money but, particularly for those with a fair amount saved already, a better strategy may be to make contributions elsewhere. This sounds counterintuitive to folks who are hyper-focused on creating a retirement nest egg, but the fact is it's probably too late to make a big difference.

The graphic below shows a 55-year-old saving $2,000 per month into their 401(k), which is already worth $1 million. This is just below the maximum amount allowed for a 55-year-old in 2022 ($20,500, plus a $6,500 "catch-up" contribution for those over 50). In 10 years' time at a conservative net return of 6%, they can expect that account balance to be twice as high. However, what would the impact be on the ending balance if we took $1,000 per month and allocated it elsewhere? As you can see, saving half as much in the second scenario doesn't have a huge impact on the results. That's because the starting balance is disproportionately impactful on the end result.

By age 55, it's a bit too late for compound interest to be your friend on new dollars saved. But let's look at scenario three. If we assume that $1,000 was reallocated into a plan that was guaranteed to rise in value, and over time provided bond-like returns without the traditional risks or taxes involved, then we can also assume the investor may feel a bit more comfortable staying invested in the market with the remainder of their assets. In general, for every 10% greater stock market exposure you've had, you've historically been rewarded with over 0.5% greater returns. (See Figure 2.1 in Chapter 2.)

Thus, if we assume 6.5% on that money due to the presence of participating whole life insurance (permission to invest), the ending balance gets much closer to what it would have been without whole life insurance. What's not shown here is that this person could *also* have well over $120,000 in cash value, bringing their combined balance above where they would have started. It's not magic, it's synergy. It's adding a strategic asset instead of blindly adding more money to an account you'll be afraid to spend from.

	Age 55 ~Max Contribution	Age 55 Halved Contribution	Age 55 Halved, More Aggressive
Starting Balance	$1,000,000	$1,000,000	$1,000,000
Monthly Savings	$2,000	$1,000	$1,000
Investment Return	6%	6%	6.5%
Years	10	10	10
Result	$2,148,794	$1,984,095	$2,081,499

Figure 9.1: The potential impact of reducing saving and increasing risk

Existing savings is another source of funding that may be more appropriate for those at or near retirement. If there aren't enough (or any) years of earned income to pay into the plan, we must look to existing savings. All participating whole life plans are created a little differently, but you can generally expect all of your contributions to be present in the plan's cash value after about 10 years, give or take, depending on whether it's designed to optimize cash accumulation or death and long-term care benefits.

Instead of thinking of it as a payment, think of it as a *cash transformation*. You'll move 10% of your cash savings into the plan each year for 10 years, and at the end of that time you'll have a much more tax-efficient, higher-yielding plan for the remainder of your life. You could also consider pulling from other savings or redirecting income into the plan. See below, where I compare maintaining a savings account over the course of your life versus reallocating it toward an overfunded whole life plan focused on growth. In the short term, you may lose a very small amount of liquidity, but the long-term cash value growth is tremendously higher, alongside death benefits that always provide greater value for your loved ones at death.

You will *never* feel comfortable spending down your emergency savings, and this dead money can be one of the biggest costs over the course of your retirement. Put it to work and get the leverage that participating whole life insurance provides.

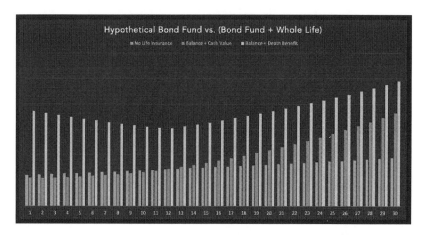

Figure 9.2: Hypothetical Bond Fund vs. Annual Shift to Whole Life

For those who may be a bit older or are much more focused on legacy, there are tremendous advantages to shifting money from risky, taxable retirement accounts into guaranteed, tax-free participating whole life insurance. At age 72, retirement accounts generally have *required minimum distributions* (RMDs), forcing you to take at least a portion of the account each year and pay any taxes due. As I reviewed in Chapter 3, this starts out relatively modest at about 3.7% of the account balance, rising to over 8.2% by age 90 and 15.6% by age 100.

Therefore, if the money is coming out one way or another, wouldn't you rather be thoughtful and strategic about it? Participating whole life insurance provides a wonderful home for those after-tax distributions, because those values rein-vested into whole life insurance will be guaranteed to grow forever and never be taxed again. The death (and LTC) benefits provide tremendous leverage on your money, and the cash value provides the backstop to your other investment and income planning.

As you can see, there's no wrong time to add participating whole life insurance to your plan. At younger ages, it has all of the benefits of life insurance, and it can be an incredible diversifier and "better bond" in your portfolio. But as you age and legacy concerns crystallize, it transforms into the most efficient way to minimize taxes over time, transfer risk outside your retirement plan and grant yourself permission to spend. Figure 9.3 below shows what it may look like to transfer about 5% of the initial account balance at age 72 into a life insurance program designed for maximum death benefit. In reality, the remaining investment account would be fluctuating in value, but the guaranteed death benefit provides enhancements to the estate along the way, while also providing a needed home for required distributions.

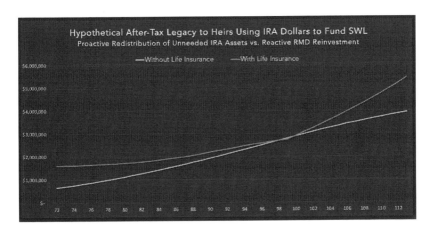

Figure 9.3: Comparison: After-Tax Legacy to Heirs

LEAVING INSTRUCTIONS

Life insurance is a love letter to your beneficiaries after you pass, demonstrating that you loved them enough to build benefits for them into your plan. But leaving a benefit without instructions can add stress and uncertainty to their lives. In most long-term relationships, one person tends to handle the finances more than the other. If you're reading this book and have made it to this point, that person is likely you. Time after time, I have heard advisors tell stories of delivering checks to beneficiaries who are grieving, stressed and clueless about what comes next. These beneficiaries are not in a place to make difficult decisions and attempt to learn concepts around financial planning and handling money. They still need to be taken care of, at least for the time being, with clear instructions and understanding on how these benefits should be allocated to accomplish goals.

The complexities of estate planning are beyond the scope of this book, but part of feeling the permission to spend comes from knowing your affairs are in order. You can get basic estate planning packages very inexpensively with various online legal services, but I highly recommend working with a local attorney to draft wills, trusts, durable powers of attorney, health-care proxies and so forth.

The more assets you have and the more complex your family dynamics are, the more you're going to want the advice of trusted counsel. These attorneys are generally using the same documents you'll get online, but spending a couple of hours discussing your hopes, dreams and unique circumstances can go a long way toward feeling like the people you love are taken care of. Additionally, establishing this relationship makes it that much easier for your loved ones to navigate complexities after your passing. Your financial advisor will likely be able to refer you to several attorneys in your area that they know and trust.

FINDING THE RIGHT ADVISOR

Choosing who to work with can make a big difference in terms of the advice you receive and which strategies get implemented. The world of financial services is very broad, and no two advisors are the same. Financial planning is more of an art than a science, and an ongoing relationship with someone acting as your guide should be what you're seeking. While these aren't a requirement, look for well-known credentials such as CFP, CLU, ChFC and RICP. Advisors with these credentials have demonstrated a commitment to continued education. These are the gold standards of the industry with rigorous curriculums one must complete. Trust and rapport are also extremely important, as this is a person you'll be working with for many years to come. If you don't immediately get the sense that they care about your success, run for the hills.

The value of a financial advisor lies in their helping you have a conversation with your future self, so that present-you makes the decisions that future-you will wish you had made. Thus, a good financial advisor asks a ton of great questions about your goals and attitudes, not just about your finances.

While financial services professionals generally all refer to themselves as advisors or planners, the truth is far more nuanced. Most begin their careers as financial salespeople, working for little to no salary and instead relying on fees and commissions to pay their bills. Insurance companies will typically pay a commission in return for an agent soliciting and placing policies. Investment companies will do the same in the form of either an upfront or ongoing percentage of assets gathered. Other advisors may not earn any commission up front but will charge a management fee as a percentage of invested assets. Finally, many advisors hold themselves out as truly objective planners, charging fees for their planning and advice without requiring that you purchase a financial product for them to get paid. These advisors, however, will typically also offer to be the representative to help you purchase insurance and investments once they have gained your trust.

Advisor bias will absolutely factor into the recommendations made. Like I said, financial planning is not science. It's the art of synthesizing complex views of the future, experiences of the past, goals, hopes, fears and a litany of unknowns into a strategy for the future that is implemented through various financial products. These products come in many categories, and within each category there are myriad choices and options. No practitioner could ever possibly know and understand them all.

Thus, advisors tend to gravitate toward the products available within the environment through which they entered the business. If they started as an insurance agent, they will most likely be focused on protection, guarantees and operating from a safety-first mentality. They will be focused on ensuring a foundation is in place with high-value contracts before reaching for lofty investment results. If they "grew up" in an investment house gathering assets and doing IRA rollovers, their focus will likely be more on wealth management, generating returns and planning based on probabilities rather than certainties. They are likely to view insurance products as commodities where the lowest current price is best, without regard for long-term value.

If this book resonates with you—and if you've made it to the end of Chapter 9, I'm guessing it does—then you're probably going to want to work with an advisor with an insurance background. In my experience, the vast majority of investors will do just fine with any advisor as long as they're saving enough money and following the general investment principles laid out in Chapter 2. In fact, countless studies have shown that passive investing via low-cost funds with minimal active management or reaction to market events is the best approach for most investors. And even if you could have done better with some other fund or investment an advisor might have recommended, that difference is extraordinarily unlikely to amount to a very meaningful sum. However, mismanaging risk can be extremely costly in the wrong circumstances and can completely derail a plan.

These days, most financial advisors operate under their own business names, so it's hard to know which companies they represent or gravitate toward. To properly implement a participating whole life insurance strategy, you're going to want to work with an advisor who represents one of the major mutual carriers with a long track record of paying high dividends. Some of these companies only sell their products through their own advisor networks, but most of the best options out there are widely available to licensed financial professionals. Don't be shy about asking which companies the advisor favors and why. If you're looking for an advisor who is certified in the strategies outlined in this book and personally vetted by me, you can visit www.permissiontospend.com to book a strategy session and get a zero-obligation review of where you're at.

Nicole and Kevin were clear on the goals they required for their children, church and charitable interests upon their eventual deaths. They determined how much risk they wanted to have covered in the event they required expensive ongoing care. They also ensured they would have at least three years of money available to spend in the event their investment portfolio was down during retirement, so it could recover. Finally, they purchased an annuity that would guarantee at least a modest level of income for life. This gave them guarantees in their plan and a level of comfort they didn't have before, with an advisor who understood all of the moving parts and would act as their coach throughout retirement.

Conclusion

You Will Be Afraid to Spend, But You Don't Have to Be

While retirement income planning comes with many risks and uncertainties, the big ones can all be planned for by proactively shifting risks during the planning process. The key is to make sure you don't just have a plan to accumulate assets but also have a thoughtful approach to how you're going to spend and enjoy them. Strategically combining insurance and investments can unlock the value of a lifetime of diligent savings and give you the optimal retirement you deserve.

We started out talking about how much you need to save to have the retirement you want. A big part of saving well for retirement, however, is managing costs and risks along the way. At younger ages, it is absolutely ok (and recommended) to be very aggressive with your investments. There are great ways to manage risk through diversified asset allocation, dollar cost averaging and periodic rebalancing. You need to know exactly what you're paying for your investments and whether you can get similar options at substantially lower costs. Furthermore, *asset location* can be one of the great

133

determinants of your success. Being mindful of the inevitability of paying taxes and spreading that tax liability out over time will be crucial to your success. Don't just blindly defer taxation until a later date, or it will come back to bite you. Roth IRAs and permanent life insurance have unique tax advantages that allow you to multiply your money many times over the course of your life and not owe any taxes.

No matter how much you're able to save, risks in retirement will cause you to cling to your hard-earned savings. You will be afraid of running out of money and will hoard some in case you need it someday. Why might you need it? Market downturns, inflation, long-term care needs and unknown longevity all combine to cast doubt on how much you should spend. Pensions, Social Security and private annuities can all help address longevity and guaranteed income concerns, but they don't guarantee a legacy to loved ones, nor extra funds in the event of declining health and expensive ongoing care. To turn your assets into a pension or strategically spend them down, you need to add guarantees to your portfolio that ensure your required outcomes occur. With a proper guaranteed backstop in place, you can know you're covered in the worst of times; but in the more likely event that all goes well, you want that backstop to also help you participate in that prosperity.

Only one asset is uniquely able to mitigate numerous risks while also providing a better way to participate in bonds. Participating whole life insurance is among the most time-tested financial vehicles in existence. It was introduced hundreds of years ago and has paid dividends from the industry's largest insurers in consecutive years since the 1860s. While other forms of permanent insurance can offer similar growth opportunities and tax advantages, they lack the guarantees that set whole life insurance apart. Through the insurance contract, you are able to participate in the returns of a diversified income portfolio while also enjoying guarantees that your money will go up at a minimum rate—all while owing nothing in taxes.

Over time, you can get bond-like returns with none of the volatility. Once you get past the early acquisition costs of the contract, you'll have a brag-worthy, safe asset earning annual returns you simply won't be able to get elsewhere on liquid, guaranteed alternatives. It's the best "boring" money can buy. Furthermore, through policy loan provisions from the right companies, you may be able to borrow at rates below the actual growth rate of the policy, allowing you to continue to earn interest while you're using money for other things.

QUALIFIED TO BE YOUR GUIDE

As I said in the beginning, I have a PhD in retirement income planning and conducted original research on whole life insurance as a fixed-income alternative under the advisement of some of the smartest minds in the field. I've had the honor and privilege to study under the most prolific researchers and authors in the field while completing a master of science in financial services, a master of business administration, a bachelor of arts in economics and the industry-leading designations of Chartered Life Underwriter (CLU) and Chartered Financial Consultant (ChFC). Academic curiosity and advising from a place of honor and integrity have always driven me to leave no difficult question unanswered.

Professionally, I have held numerous roles in the financial services industry. Starting as an award-winning financial advisor, I subsequently moved up the ranks as a product expert at a Fortune 100 company, presenting to and consulting with thousands of advisors and firm leaders in my tenure. My time at that company culminated with a senior leadership role, overseeing a 19-person team of product-marketing professionals. I worked behind the scenes with actuaries, product developers, attorneys, communications teams and sales leadership. I have been part of the decision-making process around product sustainability and maximizing the long-term value for policy owners. I have also gone toe to toe with the kinds of unscrupulous competitors and misleading marketing schemes that can give this important industry a black eye.

With 20 years of professional and academic experience, I have now refocused my career toward helping people understand the amazing benefits of what might be the most misunderstood and underappreciated asset the industry has to offer. Investments are sexy and fun to talk about, but the real magic in financial planning comes from crucial conversations around hopes, dreams, goals and what is holding people back from achieving them. As I asked questions and conducted research throughout my career, I gained an unwavering confidence and conviction in the strategies I've laid out. I hope this book instilled some of that in you, as well.

I invite you to continue your journey by visiting www.permissiontospend.com to review additional resources and subscribe. You may have been given this book by your current advisor—if that's the case, **you're in good hands** with one of the select few who "get it." If not, whether you already have a plan to review or are just getting started, we can offer you a free strategy session to review your goals and ensure you're on the right track. My network of advisors have been personally vetted by me as properly credentialed, trustworthy and knowledgeable of the concepts discussed in this book. I can honestly call most of them my friends.

Thank you for taking the time to read this book! If it's been valuable, please write a review and help others by sharing it with a friend. And of course, check out www.tomwalltalks.com for my latest content and to continue the conversation on social media.

I wish you great prosperity, continued success and permission to spend in retirement.

Tom Wall

About the Author

Tom Wall is a financial industry veteran with 20 years' experience and a PhD in retirement income planning. He has given keynote speeches to thousands of advisors from different backgrounds. He has spent most of his career as a product and strategy expert for a Fortune 100 company. Over the course of two decades, he witnessed the industry be seduced by the appeal of investments and dazzling software projections, often forsaking the core principles of planning and protection. Furthermore, as the world moved online and information became a commodity, legal departments tied licensed advisors' hands regarding what they could share—while unlicensed, uneducated, inexperienced and sometimes unscrupulous characters were free to disseminate whatever misinformation they liked.

Early in his career, Tom experienced the devastating premature loss of his mother, with subsequent losses of other close relatives, friends and clients. These people all left money, experiences and enjoyment on the table. They couldn't take it with them. This led Tom to conduct exhaustive research on how to help clients balance the spending and enjoyment of their money against saving for the future. The surprising outcome was a focus on centuries-old strategies, many of which became much more attractive in 2022 due to an act of Congress. These strategies remain some of the best-kept secrets in the industry, and Tom has emerged as one of the foremost experts in this space. Today, he hosts a study group for emerging top advisors, produces thought leadership for the industry and partners with advisors to drive client success.

Made in the USA
Middletown, DE
10 January 2024

47585152R00086